Behavioural Concerns and Autistic Spectrum Disorders

Behavioural Concerns
and Autistic Spectrum Disorders
Explorations and Strategies for Change

John Clements and Ewa Zarkowska

Jessica Kingsley Publishers
London and Philadelphia

The right of John Clements and Eva Zarkowska to be identified as authors of this work has been asserted by them in accordance with the Copyright, Designs and Patents Act 1988.

First published in the United Kingdom in 2000 by
Jessica Kingsley Publishers Ltd,
116 Pentonville Road, London
N1 9JB, England

and

325 Chestnut Street,
Philadelphia PA 19106, USA.

www.jkp.com

Library of Congress Cataloging in Publication Data

A CIP Catalog record for this book is available from the Library of Congress

British Library Cataloguing in Publication Data

A CIP Catalogue record for this book is available from the British Library

ISBN 1 85302 742 1

Printed and Bound in Great Britain by
Athenaeum Press, Gateshead, Tyne and Wear

Contents

Part 3 Making It Happen

Introduction

This book is about how people who attract autism labels can come to behave in ways that give rise to serious concerns in other people and, sometimes, themselves. It is about how to understand these behaviours and how to offer supports that enable the individual to move on from functioning in this way.

The book is written from the perspective of British trained clinical psychologists who are career specialists in the field of developmental disabilities. Our working lives focus upon people who engage in seriously worrying behaviours. Whilst we are involved with people who carry all sorts of labels, we have developed over the years a particular interest around our work for people who acquire one of the autism labels. Although we are psychologists, we are not 'therapists' in the traditional sense. It is our firm belief that everyday life is the real arena of change. If we have any useful role to play it is to develop in those involved in the everyday life of people with autism understandings and practices that will address the needs involved in 'spectacular' behaviours. It is the little and not so little things, done day in and day out, that make the difference.

This book is therefore addressed to those who support people with autism on a day-to-day basis. It is addressed to families, friends, teachers, residential staff of all kinds, voluntary supporters – whoever is there for the person over time. If other professionals and students find the book helpful that is a welcome bonus.

The ideas contained in this book are derived from many sources. We are firm believers in research and therefore some of our ideas come from the burgeoning literature in this field. We have, however, tremendous respect for the families and paid practitioners with whom we have worked over the years – we have learned a lot from them and have incorporated this learning into the book. It is important to stress that whilst we are developing a better understanding of people who get identified as autistic, there is still much that we do not understand. Thus some of the ideas in this book have a weight of evidence and experience behind them, while others are less substantiated – they seem like promising avenues, helpful ways of working but at some point will need to be properly researched. We cannot always wait for the research – the needs are urgent and action is required in the here and now. We find unhelpful professional feuding over who has the 'right answer'; and the field of autism has become notorious for such bickering. It does a serious disservice to people with autism and their families. It misrepresents seriously the current, limited state of knowledge. Our line throughout the book is to let the person with autism inform us about what is helpful. If we believe that a particular intervention may be helpful but there is not a lot of research behind it, we try to deliver it in a way that enables us to learn as objectively as possible what works for the particular individual to whom we are providing support.

The value of this book should be judged against two, linked criteria. Is the book written in a way that makes the ideas and practices understandable and accessible to the targeted readership? Second, and most important, do things get better for the people with autism who have serious behavioural issues, as a result of those who support them reading this book? We wait to hear!

Part I

Perspectives Upon The Issues

In Part I we look first at our understanding of the range of specific difficulties faced by people who get identified with one of the autism diagnoses. We try to 'unpack' the notion of autism in a way that helps to make sense of how people with this label sometimes function. The second chapter takes a broad look at behaviours that get identified as problematic – how do some behaviours and some people become identified in this way, who engages in these behaviours, what are the common contributors and what do we know in general about the process of change? A final section of this chapter tries to draw together the issues raised by looking at the topic of 'obsessions'.

We feel that reading these two chapters is essential in order to make sense of the rest of the book.

CHAPTER I

A View of Autism

What this chapter is about

This book is about the behaviours shown by people with autism that give rise to concern in other people. These behaviours are referred to variously as challenging, problematic, maladaptive or disturbed. The specific behaviours are many and varied. They include hurting other people, hurting oneself, property damage, asking the same question over and over, making personal remarks to people, masturbating in public, being awake and active all night, refusing to eat food, smearing faeces...the list is near endless. In this chapter we look at the things that we associate with the term 'autism' which may be implicated in some of these behaviours that we call challenging.

Autism – some of the struggles

The view of autism that drives this text is that autism is not something that somebody *has* – a specific problem like a virus. We see it as a means of classifying people based upon the presence of certain observable characteristics. Underlying these characteristics is a wide range of differences in how the world is experienced. In considering these differences, the reader should bear in mind the following points:

- Not everyone with the label has all these differences – individuals vary in the particular issues that they are struggling with and in the severity of the impact of the issues upon them.

- None of these differences is unique to people with this label.

- The combined effect of having several of these differences presents tremendous challenges to people labelled autistic as they endeavour to make their way in the world – challenges which cannot be underestimated.

- ○ The level of difficulty may change over time, often improvements occurring over the longer term, although sometimes difficulties becoming more pronounced from time to time and over the short term.

In what follows we seek to explore those differences and our understanding of them. We draw upon the large volume of research available, the autobiographical writings of people identified as autistic and our own experience as applied psychologists. Our current understanding is that the classification points up a large number of potential difficulties. There is no indication of a single underlying impairment. The question for us is not so much 'What is autism?' but 'How does that to which we refer as autism affect Frank/Maria/Dwayne/Imrat/Heather...?'

(A) Difficulties in understanding

Getting meaning from the flow of available information is one very broad area of difficulty for people identified as autistic. This difficulty can be broken down into a number of specific areas with which we will deal in turn.

Understanding social information

NATURE OF THE PROBLEM

Many people arrive in this world with a nervous system that is pre-set for paying special attention to people rather than to other sources of information. Attention is prioritized to faces and what people do rather than to other more general sensory input. This system has in-built design features that enable people to learn to read socially significant information from very limited input – for example, from a facial expression or a look in the eyes a judgement can be made about how a person is feeling so that one's own behaviour can be adjusted accordingly. The system is also set to learn quickly that other people's thoughts and information are different from one's own and that this needs to be taken into account so that, for example, you let them know what they do not know already and avoid boring them to death with the things that they do already know.

For people with autism this system may not be set up properly or may not develop too well. They may find it hard to pay special attention to people. When they do pay attention, they may not read the information that others do (think of it as like a reading difficulty, when someone affected cannot get meaning from the squiggles on a page that others see as letters, words, sentences and paragraphs). They may see sparkling eyes and rows of teeth but not see the underlying emotion of 'happiness'. They may notice the lines of hair or the perfume but not the facial expression. When communicating they may not notice whether the other person is bored or puzzled.

Thus a system that works automatically for many people may not work well for people with autism. In a quiet contemplative world where people mingled but essentially did their own thing, this would not matter. In a highly social world built around interrelationships and interdependence it is a real problem.

HOW THIS MIGHT RELATE TO BEHAVIOURAL DIFFICULTIES

This is illustrated best by concrete examples.

(i) The person might do something to you; for example, digging their nails into you so that red liquid (blood) appears – which is interesting or exciting for them, but painful or upsetting for you. She does not register the impact that it has upon you. Even if she grasps intellectually the effect it has on you this may still not lead her to conclude that she should not do it.

(ii) The person might completely misread your reaction to him – your pleasure might scare him, your upset excite him (see discussion of sensory difficulties).

(iii) The person might be thirsty and not grasp that she needs to communicate this to you if her discomfort is to be resolved. She becomes stuck, feeling more and more uncomfortable, and cannot grasp how to get out of this predicament. Eventually she may react to her increasing and apparently uncontrollable discomfort.

(iv) The person might go on and on about a topic that is important to him without any awareness of how this feels for the listener. He may become very upset when you try and stop him or terminate the interaction.

These few examples illustrate how the in-built difficulty in registering social information and understanding of how the world is from other people's point of view may lead the person to be careless with other people, to be frightened by other people and to be trapped in his discomforts.

Understanding language

NATURE OF THE PROBLEM

There can be a number of difficulties in extracting meaning from the stream of sound that we call language. These include:

- *Comprehension difficulties.* The person seems to have huge difficulty in understanding anything that is said. Progress is slow and often limited to just grasping the meaning of simple everyday instructions spoken in context. Even when comprehension appears to be good she may interpret very literally the language she hears.

- *Hearing difficulties.* People with autism can have a range of hearing difficulties that interfere with the ability to register and hence get meaning from language input.

- *Slowness of processing.* Some people can take on board what is being said but only at a slow rate. If too much speech is directed to them they may become agitated and start to repeat back things that are being said in an attempt to hold items in memory whilst they try to process them for meaning.

- *Developing more generalized ideas.* Even people who appear to have very good understanding of language may find it hard to go from understanding specific items to inferring more general rules. Thus the person may learn that specific acts hurt specific people and that he should not do them but he does not develop a more general rule such as 'Do unto others as you would have done unto yourself'. He may learn how to manage specific roads safely but does not develop an understanding of general principles of road safety. He may know a lot about plants and trees and where they grow but not understand why some things grow better in one place rather than another.

HOW THIS MIGHT RELATE TO BEHAVIOURAL DIFFICULTIES

(i) Serious lack of understanding of language might make the world a very unpredictable place where the person is deprived of even the most basic information coming from the flow of language. This is likely to make her very dependent upon routines, upset by changes in routines and upset by things that others find hard to understand.

(ii) Limited understanding may mean that the person misunderstands and then gets upset. When others say 'No swimming today' she may register 'swimming today', go and get her costume and towel and then get told 'No' – trouble soon follows.

(iii) Literal understanding also means that the person misunderstands and gets upset. Take the word 'bad' as an example. He may associate this with behaving in certain ways. What sense is he to make of such questions as 'Are you feeling bad?' (meaning ill or unhappy) or statements such as 'You are having a bad day today' (meaning that things are not working out successfully for you).

(iv) Slow processing may mean that the person gets overwhelmed by language and become distressed or fights to get out of extended conversational situations.

(v) Problems with abstraction mean that it is hard for the person to master certain topics, leads him to rely a lot on learning by heart, makes it hard for him to generalize. It also mean that the person's abilities can be overestimated. For example, the person has learned to ride the bus to work and therefore is thought to be independent but one day the bus is late and he has no idea what to do, becomes very upset and creates a disturbance at the bus stop. What he learned was how to get on a Number 43 bus at 7.30 am and where to get off – not how to use public transport.

Understanding time lapse and sequence

Problems with understanding social information and language are well known to both practitioners and academics/researchers. The difficulties with time lapse and sequence are well known to practitioners but less studied by the academic community.

NATURE OF THE PROBLEM

This problem involves:

- Difficulty in grasping the sense or feel of time indicators (in 5 minutes, in an hour, in a week, in a month…). The difficulty is not in the words themselves but what they signify, the expectation that they are intended to set up. Saying something will happen in 5 minutes *feels* different from saying it will happen next year – it is difficulty in that area to which we are referring.

- Difficulty in organizing the understanding of events as a sequence. This is not a general memory problem, as memory is often an area of great strength. Nor is it a language understanding problem – each of the items is well understood. Rather it is an organizational problem, a difficulty in tagging/ filing events by order or sequence in time.

HOW THIS MIGHT RELATE TO BEHAVIOURAL DIFFICULTIES

(i) Giving the person important information too far in advance may result in her becoming immediately and increasingly excited – then agitated as her whole mind is now set upon the event in question which she believes to be imminent.

(ii) Sequencing problems mean that on an everyday basis the person finds it hard to predict what will happen when, who will they see and when will they see them, when things that are important to them will happen. He may spend a lot of time worrying about it, asking people about it until others become angry.

Self awareness – understanding personal feelings, wants and needs

NATURE OF THE PROBLEM

This is another area perhaps more familiar to practitioners than to researchers. It is part of what Rita Jordan (Jordan and Powell 1995) has referred to as difficulties with the experiencing self. At one level this is a problem of understanding information that comes from within the individual. This has a double impact. It impacts upon personal experience but also impacts upon the ability to get over to other people important messages about personal wants and needs. Thus, there may be people who seem aware that they are in discomfort, know that others can help, but do not really know the nature of the discomfort that they feel – they may seem upset, grasp you by the hand or arm but then not know where to take you or what they want you to do. It is not the lack of communication skills or the lack of understanding that other people can help – it is that the person himself does not know what the problem is but is only aware that there is discomfort.

At the opposite extreme the person may fail to register some internal sensation as significant or problematic. Each year we meet at least one person who has had a serious health issue that was not in any way communicated to others (for example, someone who nearly died from a burst appendix without having expressed any signs of discomfort; someone with severely impacted wisdom teeth requiring major surgery, discovered in the course of a routine dental check). In both these examples the individuals were clearly able to experience pain and had functional verbal communication skills.

At another level there is a problem of distinguishing internal and external experience. In particular, there are some people who appear to have a problem distinguishing their own from other's emotions. They appear to experience directly the emotions of others around them. When people are angry or upset on TV they become angry or upset. On a day-to-day basis they appear to reflect closely the emotions of those people who are around them – they match hostility with hostility, anxiety with anxiety, despair with despair. They appear to absorb others' emotions like a sponge, with no capacity to reflect on the emotion and distance themselves from this.

HOW THIS MIGHT RELATE TO BEHAVIOURAL DIFFICULTIES

(i)   The person may have sensations that they cannot analyze but nevertheless experience as discomfort. To others it may just be a heart beating, a little itch, a stomach rumbling – to the person it is like a jack hammer, a tearing sensation, an impending explosion.

(ii) The person may have no way of resolving his discomforts – he does not know what they are and cannot let us know what they are. If the discomfort does not go away of its own accord or he does not get distracted then it will simply go on increasing.

(iii) The person may attribute to herself strong emotions which they witness in those around and react to these emotions in ways that others will find challenging.

(B) Difficulties in self expression

As autism is associated with a range of difficulties in making sense of incoming information, so too there are a range of difficulties in getting information over to others. The two areas are linked but not the same and individuals with this label can vary enormously in the types and combinations of specific input and output processing difficulties. Difficulties with getting information across to others can be of at least two kinds – one is a lack of awareness of the need to communicate, the other involves difficulties with the means of communicating inform-ation.

Awareness of the need to communicate

NATURE OF THE PROBLEM

Some people seem aware of their wants and needs and develop quite independent ways of sorting them out. What they seem to lack is a grasp that the other constituents of their world that we call people can be helpful in this process. They have not understood the relevance of approaching people for help. This difficulty can be apparent at a range of ability levels.

HOW THIS MIGHT RELATE TO BEHAVIOURAL DIFFICULTIES

(i)   The person may not be able to sort out his own problems, so he remains stuck with discomfort.

(ii) The person becomes determined to sort their own problems – in a way which may be quite unacceptable to others. For example, the person is thirsty so goes and helps herself to a drink – from the toilet bowl.

(iii) At a deeper level this way of functioning may have a less obvious impact. For better or worse human beings are wired to be social – to be and to join with others, to form relationships, to work together. That this is not entirely easy is obvious from how much suffering is engendered in the contexts of human relationships. It is how we are, for good and ill. Humans in isolation appear to suffer considerably. Isolation can damage our physical health and immune system, our emotional well being and our thinking and learning capacities. People with autism thus face a terrible dilemma. They have to varying degrees the human drive to be with others, the deep knowledge that survival and social interaction go together. Yet they may lack real awareness of that and the tools to effect social interaction. They may withdraw from the social world and we may be tempted to allow that to happen, to let people be in their own worlds ('their choice', after all). Yet happiness and well being do not lie that way – left to their own devices people with autism in the end become unhappy, unwell, confused and ever more driven and dominated by compulsions of one form or another. In this isolation the development of behaviours which are challenging to others becomes increasingly likely. Thus this kind of social independence is, in the end, counterproductive. In the short term it may seem impressive, particularly if the person can deal with most day-to-day situations that she encounters. In the longer term, it is our belief that such isolated independence raises the likelihood of distress and disturbance.

Difficulties with the means of communication

A much more widely accepted difficulty for some people with autism is their difficulty in acquiring a means of communicating their wants and needs.

NATURE OF THE PROBLEM

As with social understanding most infants come preset to develop communication in general and verbal language in particular. The difficulties of autism often involve a failure of these in-built mechanisms to function as well as they do for others. This may show itself in a number of ways:

- A complete failure to learn to speak or to use gesture.

- The acquisition of words early in development but which are then lost and further development appears slowed or absent.

- The acquisition of words or gestures/signs but not used in a communicative way – the mechanics but not the meaning.

- The use of words/gestures/signs to communicate about immediate personal wants and needs but not to share information (chat) or to problem solve (think).

- A slower rate of learning communication skills compared to other areas of learning.

HOW THIS MIGHT RELATE TO BEHAVIOURAL DIFFICULTIES

(i) The person may have a problem, know what it is, be unable to sort it out for himself – but be unable to get this over to us. The frustration mounts until the person either loses control of his emotions or engages in a behaviour that will grab our attention and lead us to do something which will stop the behaviour – in other words, sort the problem out. In the latter case the person has an effective solution to his problem. The trouble is that we call his solution a problem ('challenging behaviour').

(ii) Without a symbol system there are many things that it is hard
      for the person to think about and many problems that it is
      hard for her to solve. How is she to reflect on unexpected
      changes and what they mean? How does she work through
      trauma and loss?

(iii) Living without communication skills and living with all the
      other things that we mean by autism can be so fraught, so
      overwhelming that it may undermine people's learning
      capacities – perhaps they could learn some communication
      skills were it not that all their upset and distress gets in the
      way of learning.

In a number of the above discussions mention was made of the
difficulties that can arise in the areas of thinking and problem solving
and it is now time to consider these in greater detail.

(C) Some problems in thinking

Problem solving

NATURE OF THE PROBLEM

One of the early things that is noticed about children whom we identify
as autistic is that their play is different – they do not seem to engage in
imaginative play; they do not seem to create things in play, making one
thing stand for another, inventing themes and stories. Rather they
spend a lot of time doing the same thing over and over, and seem much
more interested in sensory impressions (light and dark, lines and
shadows, things that flick or spin, fluff on the carpet). If there are games
that have an imaginative element, the same game is played over and over
with little variation. Later we notice that people are very good at
routines and function very well when time is structured and things are
well organized. When routines break down, when unpredictable things
happen, when people are left to their own devices they become upset or
may behave in ways that give cause for concern.

It is as though people's minds are very dominated by sensory
experiences, are very adept at learning by rote and learning specifics. A
large amount of specific information is accumulated but extracting
general principles proves problematic. Thus when a situation is difficult

or unfamiliar – when it calls for stepping back and thinking 'What's going on here; what are my options; how can I get round this or sort this out?' – nothing happens. That system element does not kick in and the person feels trapped, stuck and all at sea. Feelings of discomfort grow and behaviour becomes disorganized or reverts to a stereotyped favourite form.

HOW THIS MIGHT RELATE TO BEHAVIOURAL DIFFICULTIES

As already suggested, not being able to access a problem-solving system can turn common, everyday occurrences into major hurdles.

(i)   Breaks in routine and transitions between situations become hard to manage and the strong feelings aroused may lead to behavioural difficulties.

(ii) Unstructured times are hard to manage. When the person has the opportunity to make a choice about what to do she finds this hard. She may therefore get bored and do something that creates excitement but which is regarded as socially unacceptable. She may revert to a stereotyped behaviour which people may regard as inappropriate.

(iii) Unpredictable events are very hard to manage. If the person is waiting for a bus that is supposed to arrive at a given time but does not, he has no means of managing that situation – it is supposed to happen, it is important that it happens, it does not happen, what to do!

(iv) Waiting times are hard to manage. The person has finished the shopping and wants to get out of the noisy crowded supermarket – that is all he can think about. He cannot get out because there is a line of people (a queue). His mind does not give him a way of distracting himself and filling in the time he has to wait.

(v)   Choices are hard to manage. When someone says 'What do you want?' the person is supposed to be able to think of the options, narrow them down to the legal and the feasible, check out how he feels and make a response accordingly. If this does not happen the person gets upset because he knows people want him to say something but he does not know what to say. He may say a word which is easy for him to say and end up with something that he does not want. He may say something which is the word for a thing that he always wants but then gets told that he cannot have that. All these are routes to challenging outcomes – from a 'simple' question of choice.

Tightly focused attention

NATURE OF THE PROBLEM

For many people their minds can process simultaneously more than one line of information. Thus you may be focused upon reading this text but are aware of the time and what you will be doing next; you are also monitoring background sights and sounds and will certainly pick up anything of personal significance (mention of your name, someone asking if you want a coffee). On the other hand many people will also have the experience of being so absorbed in a task that everything else is blocked out (as you get more and more absorbed in reading you may lose track of time, miss the sound of the door opening or closing). However, there is also for most people the sense that we have some control over how our attention resources are deployed. For some people with autism this flexible, multi-channel deployment of attention appears to be problematic.

- Attention may be unfocused. The person may be unable to filter out redundant information and focus on what is relevant at the time. Everything is bombarding him simultaneously.

- Attention may be so tightly locked to a topic/task/sensation that all other information is blocked out.

There appears to be only a two-way switch, an all or nothing approach, rather than a slider/dial control (this image recurs in our understanding of the experience of people with autism).

HOW THIS MIGHT RELATE TO BEHAVIOURAL DIFFICULTIES

(i) Without focus the person gets overwhelmed by all the incoming information and may become very distressed.

(ii) When focus is locked to 'target' the person may fail to notice any other information and may therefore get caught by surprise when changes occur, when she needs to stop and do something else, when something of significance to her intrudes. This in turn may precipitate very high levels of upset for reasons not easy for outsiders to understand.

Binary thinking

NATURE OF THE PROBLEM

The two-way switch analogy was mentioned above and we do see this as a more general characteristic of some people with autism (and, indeed, of some without). When reflecting upon events or experiences they are not able to rate them on a continuous or multi-point scale (from *terrible* to *wonderful*). Instead they are either *OK* or *not OK*, *good* or *bad* – no in-between. This kind of perfectionism can be extremely punishing to live with. The person, his work, his life, everybody around him, the kind of day he is having can be judged in only one of two ways, no shades of grey, no ambivalence, no gradations.

HOW THIS MIGHT RELATE TO BEHAVIOURAL DIFFICULTIES

(i) Low tolerance of things being less than perfect may mean that the person will destroy a piece of work where she perceives the slightest mistake. She may regard herself as a complete failure. It becomes dangerous to correct her. The person becomes dangerous to herself if she fails to meet these standards.

(ii) Inability to perceive situations and outcomes using a graduated system of evaluation means that if things are not going well for the person, this is perceived as a complete disaster, with all the accompanying, highly intense feelings that such an interpretation evokes.

Mental/behavioural stuttering (perseveration)

NATURE OF THE PROBLEM

This is similar to tightly focused attention but involves the issue of control. Everyone has the experience of thinking that occurs without a sense of personal control – daydreaming, ruminating, getting distracted. Some people experience this very powerfully in the form of compulsions. Much of the time, however, we have the sense of being able to focus and control our mental processes. For some people with autism there is much less confidence in this sense of control. A task or topic may be focused upon but it then gets hard to stop – the topic or task is repeated over and over and there seems no way of stopping it unless someone intervenes – no pause or stop button that the person is able to operate for herself.

HOW THIS MIGHT RELATE TO BEHAVIOURAL DIFFICULTIES

(i) The person may get stuck, repeating the same thing over and over and becoming more and more distressed at this experience.

(ii) The person may get stuck repeating the same thing over and over and other people get very angry with him.

(D) The world of personal sensations – sensory, physical and emotional difficulties

Problems with sensory modulation

NATURE OF THE PROBLEM

Although over or under responsiveness to environmental stimuli is a well known characteristic of autism it is not clear exactly how this is to be understood. It is included in this section because of the impact that sensitivity can have upon the person. Some people with autism become very distressed in the presence of certain sounds, sights (colours, space, movement in the visual field) and touches. We are less sure about tastes and smells. The specific sensory inputs that create disturbance vary across individuals and individuals can vary over time in how distressed they become by their sensitivities. The inputs in question are things that most other people take for granted and process without discomfort.

Some of these sensitivities are more clearly recognizable as phobias. Thus some people with autism, like others, may find the presence of dogs or wasps, for example, very aversive. Whether phobias and sensory discomforts should be regarded as separate issues is not clear at present.

HOW THIS MIGHT RELATE TO BEHAVIOURAL DIFFICULTIES

(i)   The sensory difficulties will mean that there are triggers for distress that others may not understand or appreciate – certain everyday situations become very aversive for the person and escape/avoidance/attack behaviours may be activated.

Problems with physical well being

NATURE OF THE PROBLEM

There is controversy and uncertainty as to whether there are some health issues that are especially linked to autism (for example, difficulties in breaking down certain food stuffs such as gluten or casein, gut infections or leakages, difficulties in immune system functioning). From a practitioner perspective, however, some people seem very vulnerable to general infections and others have recurrent health issues such as ear infections, asthma or hay fever, skin problems, bowel problems.

HOW THIS MIGHT RELATE TO BEHAVIOURAL DIFFICULTIES

(i)   Any unwellness will reduce the person's tolerance and increase her irritability and this will raise the general likelihood of encounters that others will identify as challenging.

(ii) The person may have learned that one way to deal with pain is to self inflict another powerful sensation – this may block the pain directly through some form of distraction or indirectly by triggering the release of the body's internal painkillers (the endogenous opiates).

(iii) More controversially, it has been suggested that when the person eats certain things a breakdown error produces something like an opiate. This may generate fluctuating levels of opiate-like chemicals in the brain (a bit like 'injection-withdrawal') with accompanying physical and emotional discomfort.

Problems with emotional well being

NATURE OF THE PROBLEM

Some people show much greater general evidence of negative rather than positive feelings – their fight/flight systems are much more readily activated than their pleasure systems, their thoughts and memories are dominated by negative themes, they do not laugh very much. People will also vary in the intensities of their emotional experience – their emotionality. These are matters of temperament/personality but constitute a vulnerability for people whose experience may be dominated by intense negative emotionality (that is, there may be a powerful interaction between personality type and the experience of autism in our society). There are some who appear to have difficulties in emotional modulation – in limiting increases in emotionality. They become excited, happy, upset, angry but then appear to have no means of putting a cap on the increase in emotional tone and become more and more extreme in their emotions until sometimes they lose control.

Some people show distinct cycles, especially down phases, when general mood and tolerance is reduced, interest is lost and sometimes eating and sleep are affected – this will lead some to being diagnosed by psychiatrists as depressed. Some will also be diagnosed with obsessive-compulsive disorder – certain rituals and routines take on a driven quality, accompanied by negative emotions and explosive responses to any attempt to curtail the ritual. In some the cycles will go from high to low and this may lead to a diagnosis of bi-polar disorder.

A small number of people at all levels of ability show a marked breakdown in adolescence or early adult life. This may involve withdrawal from activities, a loss of skills, intense negative emotions (anger being particularly prominent), a refusal to accept limits on oneself and/or the imposition of ever more tyrannical rules on others. This phase may last for an extended period of time (some years).

HOW THIS MIGHT RELATE TO BEHAVIOURAL DIFFICULTIES

(i) A temperamental style that involves frequent intense negative emotionality might be a factor in the origin of behavioural difficulties. Upsets of any kind may generate strong motivations to escape. These strong motivations may shape up behaviours that successfully lead to escape or other important results. The behaviours becomes useful and effective and this leads to them continuing.

(ii) Problems with emotional modulation mean that emotions get out of control, arousal levels go on increasing unchecked until the emotional state becomes aversive even though it may have started as a positive experience (I laugh till I cry).

(iii) Lack of emotional well being, whether cyclical or part of a breakdown, certainly sets the scene for many problematic behaviours – it reduces general tolerance and brings out escape/avoidance feelings in a range of situations especially where pressures or demands are being placed upon the person.

(iv) A refusal to accept limits and the imposition of rules on others may trigger violent confrontations with the world around.

(v) Breakdown may be accompanied by very negative beliefs about oneself (I am a hopeless/worthless/bad person) or others (it's your fault that things are not right for me) which can contribute to behaviours which damage the self or others.

(vi) Lack of emotional well being may be accompanied by an increase in compulsive behaviours and attempts to interrupt these rituals will trigger very challenging responses.

(vii) Lack of emotional well being may also be accompanied by increased difficulties in controlling body movements and this might be very problematic to others (see Part II).

It is our view that the lack or loss of well being (emotional or physical) is one of the most important contributors to people with autism acting in ways that others find challenging.

(E) Control of physical movements

NATURE OF THE PROBLEM

Although some people with autism are beautifully coordinated, others are not. Indeed it is almost a defining feature of the people who have a diagnosis of Asperger's syndrome that they are clumsy. Many people with autism show behaviours which we call stereotypies – rocking, flicking, flapping, twirling, bouncing movements. In some people these occur on an everyday basis. In others they accompany increases in arousal. More recently two major problems in relation to the voluntary control of movement have been identified as associated with autism.

The first involves a difficulty with inhibiting movements. Some movements seem to be tic-like, to have a life of their own so that the individual does not feel able to control them. There has been an association noted between autism and one of the better-known movement disorders, Tourette's syndrome. More elaborate movement sequences can also have a compulsive element and feel out of control to the individual. It is believed that there may be some common neurological ground between tics and compulsions.

The second area of difficulty involves the initiating of movements. Some people with autism seem to develop fixed postures and get stuck, seemingly unable to move. Some autobiographical writings comment upon this and clinicians have noted similarities with Parkinson rigidities and the catatonias evident after the major encephalitis lethargica epidemic in Europe in the 1920s.

HOW THIS MIGHT RELATE TO BEHAVIOURAL DIFFICULTIES

(i) Through mechanisms that are not yet well understood there appears to be an association between tic disorders, compulsions and some types of self-injury and aggression. High levels of stress raise the frequency of uncontrolled movements.

(ii) Frozen postures may be interpreted as attention seeking or non-compliance and trigger hostile reactions which set off a train of events resulting in the person with autism being identified as challenging.

Lest we forget

In our discussion of differences in the way that people with the label of autism experience their world, we should remember that not all of these differences are problematic for them. Indeed, some of these differences in experiencing the world may be quite advantageous. Problems with social understanding may mean that a person is less susceptible to social influence and pressures for conformity. She is less likely to lie, less likely to develop stereotypes, prejudicial or otherwise. Freedom from language may enable her to devote more attention to other aspects of the world and human capacity – to see the world in different ways and notice things that others fail to notice, to enter more easily the domains of music and visual representation. Focusing very tightly on a topic or activity and practising it over and over without the mind wandering off may enable her to develop outstanding talents – not just for music, for drawing, for complex mathematical calculations but also for some of those exquisite hand movements and capacities to spin, flick and balance that others are quite unable to manage. This way of a mind working also makes it possible for her to be incredibly reliable in structured and predictable situations. Finally, whilst it is true that the human capacity to read other people has enabled the species to evolve in very successful ways, it is that same capacity that gifts us with stereotypes and prejudices whose behavioural manifestations range from discrimination to genocide. There is much to be said for the patient accumulation of data and the active inhibition of the rush to judgement.

Concluding remarks

We have tried to present here how some of the things that we associate with the term autism may be implicated in behaviours that we call challenging. In doing so we have deliberately avoided endorsing one specific theory of autism and rushing to judgement about a core underlying impairment from which all the specific difficulties derive. At this stage in our understanding of autism we prefer to approach the issues in a fragmented way and be open to the possibility in the future of a radically different way of understanding the nature of what we now call autism.

We have, therefore, deliberately chosen to discuss autism in terms of a large number of specific difficulties, with the challenge being to find out for each individual the exact difficulties that he or she is struggling with. Not everyone classified as autistic will have all these difficulties – indeed maybe no one has all these difficulties. Appendix I provides a checklist to help identify the most significant issues for the person(s) that you know.

By approaching the issues in a more fragmented way, we are better able to identify for any one individual the difficulties which she experiences and to target those difficulties. However, whilst holding to a preference for specifics it is also clear to us that these specific areas do interact to produce the outcomes that we call challenging.

Our personal struggle is to understand autism as a different way of being in the world and we see the work as finding ways of supporting those who are different. Our target is the distress caused by differences rather than the differences themselves. Our task is to alleviate the distress. Some of what we do will be helping those *with* the label to learn and know more. Some of what we do will be to help those *without* the label to understand and accommodate to fellow citizens who see things differently.

CHAPTER 2

Beyond Autism – Understanding Human Behaviour

What this chapter is about

In Chapter 1 we looked at how the characteristics associated with autism may increase the vulnerability of a person to behave in ways that others find challenging – such characteristics reflecting ways of perceiving and interpreting the world which may be at odds with how others without autism labels perceive and understand the world. In this chapter we look more generally at human behaviour, particularly those behaviours which may be considered challenging or unacceptable. We will consider how we come to make judgements that someone's behaviour may be 'challenging' and the factors which may play a part in determining our responses to such behaviours on a day-to-day basis. We will discuss the various influences which need to be taken into account if we are to make sense of a person's behaviour and, in turn, plan better and more comprehensive ways to support those who show such behaviours.

Identifying behaviour as challenging

This is an important issue. Identifying someone's behaviour as challenging is not a straightforward process. There is no generally accepted 'list' of behaviours to which we automatically attach this label. Making judgements about others' behaviour is not an objective, scientific diagnosis, it is a social judgement. Identification depends upon a number of factors, most of which are quite subjective.

(1) Different people have different tolerance levels for different behaviours. Thus whilst one person may be able to block out continual screaming and may not therefore consider it a problem, another may find this sound to be extremely wearing and intrusive and hence be very challenged by it. It is not as straighforward as this, however. Personal tolerance levels fluctuate depending on a person's mood, the stresses she is under, her physical health, and so on. This means that whilst most days the continual screaming poses no problem for the person, on some days she has very little or zero tolerance for it.

(2) We each have personal standards for behaviour. For example, some people find it unacceptable that others might swear at them or be verbally abusive. Others may find this way of interacting with others perfectly acceptable – it does not present a problem for them.

(3) Our acceptance of certain behaviours may be linked to our value systems. For example, some people will see people with disabilities as generally oppressed within society and will value highly a disabled person who can stand up for herself if bullied or pressured, even if the form her behaviour takes is socially unacceptable (for example, physical aggression). Others may not value such behaviour, however, and label it 'challenging'. They may place greater value on conformity and compliance even if this is at the cost of the person's own well being, which in turn may link to deeper beliefs about people with disabilities as a threat to the social order.

(4) Our personal attitudes towards and relationship with the person are likely to influence our judgements about his behaviour. If we like and respect a person and he behaves inappropriately we are more likely to find a justifiable, external explanation of his behaviour (someone upset him). If we do not like or respect the person, we are more likely to interpret his behaviour as being due to internal factors (he's spiteful).

It is clear, therefore, that no two people are likely to view another person's behaviour in the same way. Indeed, any one individual is likely view another person's behaviour differently on different days and at different times. And yet this apparently simple judgement – is it or is it not a problem – will have important consequences for the person because it will have a major influence on other people's response to his behaviour. If the behaviour is judged to be unacceptable or challenging the response is likely to be very different from a response based upon a judgement that the behaviour is acceptable. Such social judgements need special care, particularly when made by powerful people about those who are less powerful and who cannot argue with those judgements. On the basis of such judgements the individual may find himself moving house, changing jobs, ingesting mind and body altering medications.

It is therefore helpful to operate some checks when the behaviour of a person whom we are paid to support is being identified as problematic and as the focus for efforts at change. The type, frequency and intensity of a behaviour are all likely to influence the decision that there is a problem to address. As a check on whether attempts at change are justified, we suggest the following criteria be used to help the decision:

(1) The behaviour should be such that it is levying or likely to levy a significant cost upon the individual (the cost might be physical – damage or injury; the cost might be social – imprisonment, banning from important places or activities).

(2) The behaviour should be such that it is levying or likely to levy a significant and unreasonable cost upon others (costs might be physical – injury, damage to personal property; costs might be personal – loss of sleep, persistent stress).

It is important, also, when there is any question of a behaviour being officially identified as causing concern to look at the quality of relationships around the individual to see how that might be influencing the judgements being made.

Responding to behaviour

This issue, too, is more complex than would appear at first sight. How we respond to a person's behaviour is likely to dependent upon a number of factors. The first, as we have said, is the subjective judgement of whether or not we consider it to be a problem. However, there are other factors too.

(1) Judgements or theories about the reason behind another person's behaviour are likely to have a major influence on people's response to it. Making judgements about other people's behaviour is instinctive to most people. The problem is that most of these judgements tend to be very simple, involving a single cause – and responses tend to be based upon these judgements. If the theory is very simple the response, too, is likely to be simple. Thus if we believe that the reason for the person spitting is 'attention seeking' our intervention plan may be simply to ignore the behaviour. If we believe that a person's scratching is caused by the person being spiteful, our intervention plan may be simply to reprimand or punish the person.

(3) The emotions engendered by a behaviour are likely to play an important role. If people are frightened or repulsed by a behaviour they may respond in a way that reflects these emotions (for example, avoidance of the person, attempts to control her in order to compensate for the fear, giving in to her). If people find a behaviour amusing they may respond with attention and laughter – they may encourage her.

(3) Personal feelings that people hold towards the person are another important factor. A response to the behaviour of a person we like and whom we value is likely to be very different from the way we respond to the same behaviour of a person whom we dislike or have little respect for. If we like and respect the person our response is more likely to involve a greater degree of empathy, more negotiation in order to reach a compromise, whereas our response to the behaviour of a person we do not like or respect is more likely to be punitive and aimed at rapid control (see also above).

(4) People's responses to the behaviour of others may be driven
     by personal needs. Such personal needs may include a need to
     impress or to appear competent in front of colleagues, a need
     always to be in control. These personal needs have little to do
     with the needs of the person himself and the responses they
     trigger may not be in his best interests.

To respond to behaviour in helpful ways, therefore, requires an exam-
ination of our own thoughts, attitudes and beliefs. It also requires us to
look more objectively at people's behaviour so that fair and helpful
judgements can be made. Having identified and agreed that there is a
problem to address we need then to look to a process of careful
assessment which assembles objective information so that a story
emerges about the behaviour – a story which identifies a whole range of
factors which may be influencing its occurrence either directly or
indirectly.

About human behaviour

People with autism labels are essentially just like others without such
labels. Their behaviours adhere to the same 'laws' as do all of our
behaviours. Therefore in considering the behavioural difficulties which
people with autism may present, it is necessary to be mindful of certain
important facts about human behaviour in general.

(1) Behaving in ways that trouble others or cause problems for
     others is part of the human condition. It is not something
     special to people with autism. Everyone does it – sometimes
     in very damaging ways, sometimes in minor ways.

(2) Most behaviours, whether identified by others as problematic
     or not, are meaningful. They are about meeting needs and
     wants.

(3) Behaviour is not random. We all learn which behaviours are
     most effective in meeting personal wants and needs and the
     circumstances under which these behaviours are most likely to
     be effective. We learn this by the responses and outcomes
     which our behaviours achieve for us over time. Over time we
     will come to rely more heavily upon those behaviours which

achieve most quickly and with least effort the outcomes that are important to us.

(4)   Some behaviours which people show are associated with high emotionality. These behaviours may not be meeting the person's needs or desires – they are merely expressions of a high level of emotion, sometimes bringing relief and sometimes not. The notion of threshold may be helpful here. When we pass a certain point of arousal (upset or excitement; see Chapter 3) we may no longer be able to inhibit certain behaviours. Individuals will vary in the strength of their inhibitions and the absolute point on the arousal curve when the threshold is exceeded.

(5)   People's behaviour varies over time. People's needs and wants vary. They may be more challenging at certain phases in their lives (terrible twos, stroppy adolescents, miserable mid-lifers, grumpy old age pensioners). They may be more challenging under particular circumstances – for example, when encouraged by peers, when unwell, when feeling stressed, lonely and unloved, when feeling trapped, when under the influence of alcohol or drugs.

(6)   People do not 'grow out of' or 'get cured' once and for all of their behaviours. 'Challenging' behaviour is not an illness, it is a way of coping with day-to-day pressures, a way of meeting everyday needs. As the pressures on a person increase and his coping resources become stretched, as his needs become more intense and pressing, so the risk of using more extreme behaviours increases.

(7)   The reasons behind one person's behaviours are not necessarily the same as the reasons behind another person's, even though the behaviour may take the same form. One person might shout and throw things because she is overwhelmed with frustration, another might engage in the same behaviours because he wants to be noticed, he wants people to listen.

(8) The likelihood of behaving in ways which are troublesome
     and problematic is reduced if people live lives adapted to their
     personal wants and needs and if they have good coping skills
     and resources upon which they can call when the going gets
     tough.

Developing an understanding of an individual's behaviour

We have said that the reasons behind one person's behaviour are not
usually the same as the reasons behind another person's behaviour. The
reason why one person hurts others is not the same as the reason why
another does so. Each person is different and each behaviour needs to
be considered in its own right. In addition, the reasons behind one
behaviour may not be the same as the reasons behind another behaviour which the person shows. A person may shout because this
makes others do as he asks. He may hit because this makes others leave
him alone. There is therefore a need to build a detailed understanding
of why a particular person is engaging in a particular behaviour and
why he is likely to engage in that behaviour more under some
circumstances than under others.

The explanation of a person's behaviour will probably reflect more
than a single cause – behaviours tend to reflect the operation of several
contributory factors rather than single causes. Behind every behaviour
that a person shows lies a story – a story about the person, the world she
lives in and the day-to-day interaction between her and her world. The
more elements of this 'story' that we can identify the more avenues will
be open to us for supporting her in constructive ways. Some of the
important factors which can influence behaviour and which we may
need to understand when trying to make sense of a person's behaviour
are outlined below. They are summarized in Appendix 2.

(1) Most behaviour is functional. Thus one factor to consider is
     in what way the behaviour is functional for the person – what
     does it achieve for him. On at least some occasions, does it
     achieve access for him to something he wants or needs –
     human contact, a particular activity, a basic human need,
     sensory pleasure, a sense of control? Does it achieve, on some
     occasions, escape or postponement of something he does not

want – human contact, a particular task or activity, relief from discomfort or an aversive sensory experience?

(2) Most behaviours are triggered by an external or internal event. Thus a second factor to consider is what might be triggering the behaviour – the things which seem to set it off. These may be identifiable stimuli in the external environment – noise, crowding, a request, a denial, the sight of something that the person wants. They may be invisible – the thoughts, interpretations, feelings or physical sensations that she experiences.

(3) Behaviours do not occur continually. They are more likely to occur under certain conditions. Thus another very important factor to consider is the circumstances under which the behaviour is more (or less) likely to occur – the probability of the behaviour. Certain conditions increase the probability of behaviour because they decrease the person's tolerance and ability to cope effectively with day-to-day stressors. Such conditions may be external or internal. They include activities which the person is asked to engage in, certain physical environments that he finds himself in, other people and their attitudes, his lifestyle (meaningful occupation, money, independence, choice, relationships), his physical and mental health at the time, recent significant events (for example, moves, losses, accidents), the life stage which he has reached, his general understanding of what is expected and what is going on around him.

(4) Behaviours are skills which the person has learned to use to achieve important outcomes. Thus her skills are another significant factor to consider. If a person lacks or has limited communication skills then she may have no appropriate way of communicating her needs and wants to others – using 'challenging' behaviour may be the only option. If a person lacks the skills to occupy himself, then he may constantly seek out others, because others provide him with stimulation and occupation. Alternatively he may develop a preference for sensory stimulation (such as rocking, finger flicking) as an

alternative form of occupation. If a person lacks social skills and social problem-solving skills (how do I deal with this situation which I have got myself into with this person) he will experience problems adapting or adjusting his behaviour in difficult social situations. If he lacks self-control skills, he will have difficulty controlling high levels of emotion.

(5) People and their behaviours have a history. Another important factor to take into account, therefore, is historical information about the person and her world. What are her likes and dislikes; are there any traumas, life events which have occurred which she has not yet resolved and which may be adversely affecting her emotional well being? What have her early learning experiences been like – how has she been taught to interact with others, to meet her needs?

(6) The ways that people perceive and understand the world have a significant influence upon their behaviour. We need to know how the person experiences the world. For the person with autism this is likely to be different in some respects from the ways in which others experience their world (see Chapter 1). This may increase her vulnerability to behaving in socially unacceptable or otherwise challenging ways.

In understanding the behaviour of people with autism we always struggle with these various perspectives – what is to do with autism, what is to do with the people that they are and the options for behaving in the situation, what is to do with the life that they lead and the social world of which they are a part, what is to do with the history that they have and what is to do with the pressures of the moment. In answering the question 'Why does this behaviour happen?' some of the factors will be to do with autism, some will not. We need to think in terms of multiple contributors not single causes.

Thus, a person may be hypersensitive to auditory stimuli, the presence of which trigger distress behaviours. On good days she may be able to cut the sound out. Tolerance to such stimuli may be decreased, however, when she is tired or unwell or confused by new surroundings or in crowded environments. If she is unable to communicate what is distressing her or if she is unable to escape from the aversive situation, if others do not understand her difficulties, and admonish her for not co-operating with activities or requests at this time, her anxiety and distress will increase and her ability to cope with demands that are being placed upon her will decrease further. She may become aggressive or self-injurious or show some other form of problematic behaviour. Others may then respond to these behaviours by taking her from the situation to calm her down. Thus there is a positive outcome to her behaviour and the likelihood of her using the same behaviour in similar situations in the future is increased.

Making changes

Just as there are likely to be several contributors to a person's problematic behaviour so too there will be many contributors to his positive well being and positive behaviour. In order for him to function in socially appropriate and constructive ways he needs to have a number of resources, both personal and external. These resources include:

- Skills and knowledge (for example, being able to communicate, understanding the consequences of one's actions, understanding other people, problem solving, independence skills, social skills and skills of self control)
- Good physical health
- Positive mental health
- A good place to live
- Meaningful occupation, work
- Good quality social supports
- Meaningful social relationships
- Being valued and respected
- Having some control over his life
- A life adapted to his particular needs.

The broad outline of the approach taken in this book is that working with the behavioural challenges that people present to us is not about trying directly to eliminate behaviour but about extending and building upon the conditions that enable them to function socially in a constructive way. This means:

(1) Enhancing and building personal resources to help the person deal with the pressures of everyday life and the additional pressures that come from understanding the world in a different way.

(2) Enhancing quality of life – a quality of life which may be adversely affected by the person having a learning disability, and understanding the world in different ways – in ways which we call autistic – and responding to her differences in ways others find unacceptable, frightening, anxiety provoking or irritating. A quality of life that may be affected adversely by the attitudes of others and of society at large.

We will use a discussion of the topic of obsessions to illustrate the importance of building understanding of the behaviour for each individual and how this understanding may help to develop appropriate interventions.

Obsessions – some illustrative stories

One of the major concerns raised by those who live and work with people whom we identify as autistic is 'obsessions'. The person has an activity that he does over and over again, that takes up a lot of everyone's time and that can lead to great confrontations when attempts are made to stop or curtail the behaviour – whether it is spinning things, juggling things, flushing things down the toilet, collecting laces or newspapers, particular videos, asking the same question over and over, going on endlessly about power stations or music from the 1960s. Although people who do not have autism tend to label all these things by a single word – obsessions – there appear to be four distinct themes. You can only know which best applies to a behaviour of concern by detailed knowledge of the individual and an understanding of what the behaviour means to that person – you cannot know just by the form that a behaviour takes. The four themes are related to the function that the behaviour has for the person.

Hobbies and passions

THE FUNCTION OF THESE BEHAVIOURS

These are behaviours that are repeated because they produce a positive outcome for the person. She loves seeing things that way, listening to the answer to that question, talking about that topic, doing that particular activity. These things may be highly annoying to everyone else but for her they are a source of delight.

OTHER SIGNIFICANT CONTRIBUTING FACTORS

Given that the person is less interested in social relationships she is free to enjoy the sensory world. She develops these interests readily and given that her mind tends to stick on topics she does the same thing over and over. Her difficulty in taking a social perspective means that she is not inhibited by what other people think about her or by their feelings when she involves them in her favourite pastime. Trouble arises when others try to stop the person and she does not want to stop. It can also arise when the person gets stuck – much though she loves this activity she does sometimes want to do something else but can find herself unable to stop and gets distressed by this. She is more likely to engage in the behaviour when she is left alone for long periods or given a lot of 'free' unstructured time.

SUPPORTING THE PERSON

This is likely to involve several strategies. These may include channelling the interest into a constructive activity or occupation; ensuring that the person has alternative interesting things to do; providing a high level of structure to ensure that he does not spend all of his time on his 'hobby'; helping him cope with stopping the activity and helping him to understand that stopping does not mean for ever – that he can return to the activity later; placing boundaries on the activity if it is intrusive upon others and supporting him to accept those boundaries; helping those supporting him to understand the importance of the behaviour to him.

Rituals

THE FUNCTION OF THESE BEHAVIOURS

These are things that the person likes to be just so (arrangements of objects, ways of doing things). We all have such rituals – they are an important part of human life. The motivation is mixed – rituals bring some pleasure but also some reassurance and security – they keep the world a safe place. It is only a problem if they intrude unreasonably upon others or are so extensive that they interfere demonstrably with the quality of life for the individual.

OTHER SIGNIFICANT CONTRIBUTING FACTORS

The person's lack of social perspective may lead him to intrude his rituals unreasonably on to others. Or he may develop such extensive rituals that others will see that his quality of life is impaired. The rituals are increased when he becomes anxious. Anxiety occurs when there are many changes in staff, when activities are frequently cancelled; when he is left unsupported for long periods of time; when people label these behaviours as obsessional and do not respect their importance in anxiety reduction, and intrude unreasonably on his preferred way of doing things.

SUPPORTING THE PERSON

Again, support is likely to be multifaceted. It may include providing a lifestyle which is secure and predictable so that the person feels reassured and anxiety free; providing her with plenty of other pleasurable activities; ensuring that she is not left unsupported for long periods of time; finding more direct ways to help her manage her anxiety (for example through regular exercise); placing sensitive boundaries upon the rituals to ensure that they do not intrude upon her quality of life nor on the quality of life of others; helping those supporting her to understand and to respect her rituals.

Worries

THE FUNCTION OF THESE BEHAVIOURS

Worries are things that concern the person – such as the weather, or who she is working with today. They are generally a source of mild discomfort. They are always there and sometimes they get out of control and the person becomes very upset. The person seeks to relieve the discomfort through behaviour that others might find irritating (for example, going on and on about the thing that is worrying her, asking the same question over and over).

OTHER SIGNIFICANT CONTRIBUTING FACTORS

The person is concerned about her worries and tends to dwell upon them. This itself is not a problem. The difficulty is that the person cannot problem-solve too well. It is hard for her to work out how to distract or to calm herself once she has started to focus on a topic. Her tendency to stick at things keeps her trapped in her concern with no way out. Thus a minor worry can build up and up and culminate in a large outburst. Worries may become more intense if her mood is low.

SUPPORTING THE PERSON

Support will take a number of forms. This may include providing reassurance for the person; providing him with direct coping strategies to use when the worries start to become distressing; alleviating the low mood; keeping him occupied so he is distracted from his worries; ensuring that when the worry gets too much and the person loses control, we can keep him and others safe.

Compulsions

THE FUNCTION OF THESE BEHAVIOURS

These are things that people *must* do – or they feel that something terrible will happen (they *must* go back and forth through the door so many times, they *must* go and slap that particular person on the back so many times, they *must* remove those items from the wall, they *must* let their arm make a particular movement). The function of the behaviour is that it makes the person feel temporarily less uncomfortable – but then he starts to feel uncomfortable again and so has to repeat the behaviour. He may have a strong sense that he cannot control this behaviour although he may try very hard to do so (sit on his hands, sit in a corner blocked in by a table, hide under a blanket).

OTHER SIGNIFICANT CONTRIBUTING FACTORS

The person may have considerable experience of his body not always acting in the ways that he intends – sometimes it will do things that he does not want it to do, sometimes it will not do things that he does want it to do. Likewise his mind – thoughts come into his mind without him deliberately thinking about that topic. He may also have dislikes or worries – things that he finds hard to tolerate but will put up with when things are going well. These experiences get heightened when he loses his sense of well being, when he becomes depressed. He becomes filled with negative thoughts, his body is less and less in control, dislikes become more and more painful or perceptually disturbing – and he must do those things that produce immediate, if temporary, relief: nothing and no-one will stand in his way. Others become angry with him, do not understand his difficulty controlling his behaviour and see it as 'deliberate' or 'spiteful'. They do not recognize his genuine attempts to control the behaviour and see this as 'non compliance' or 'opting out'.

SUPPORTING THE PERSON

As with other behaviours there will be many levels of support. These may include direct attempts to improve the low mood; teaching the person a self-control strategy; placing some external control on the behaviour if she is unable to control it herself; changing the attitudes and understanding of those supporting her.

Our aim in discussing the possible factors involved in behaviours that we label as 'obsessions' and the management of these behaviours has been to illustrate a number of points.

(1) Behaviours referred to by a single general term are not all the same, they have different personal meanings. We therefore need to define clearly the behaviour of concern.

(2) Having defined the behaviour clearly we need then to strive towards an understanding of the personal meaning of the behaviour for the individual – this means knowing the various factors which may be interacting to produce the behaviour.

(3) Providing appropriate support for the person will follow from understanding the various factors which may be operating. It will involve developing intervention strategies to address as many of these factors as possible.

(4) The goal of the work is to address the person's well being, his coping resources and his quality of life. The goal is not simply the direct reduction or elimination of the behaviours of concern. When the contributing factors have been addressed there should be some decrease in the behaviour, at least to the extent that it does not intrude upon the life of the person or the lives of others.

Concluding remarks

Behaving in ways that others identify as 'challenging' or problematic is not exclusive to people with autism. It is part of being human. Most of our behaviours reflect attempts to meet our needs, satisfy our desires, cope with frustrations and high levels of emotion. For those with the label of autism there may be an increased vulnerability to show such behaviours. The world is so much more difficult for them to understand and the coping strategies which they use are often unacceptable to others and may be limited by a lack of personal resources, such as problem solving skills and flexibility. Their motivations and priorities may be different from the motivations and priorities of others. Constructive help and support will require that we attempt first to understand as much as possible about the various factors which may be operating to produce and maintain the behaviour in question and from this understanding to develop a comprehensive package of supports.

Such a package may need to address a number of areas of the person's life – not just her particular vulnerabilities which arise from the different way the person with autism experiences her world. It may also need to address the person's well being, her skills and competencies, her social supports, her safety and the safety of others.

Part II

Helpful Practices

The eight chapters in this part detail the range of needs that may be implicated in behaviours that cause concern and ways of working to meet those needs. Whilst we hope that readers will go through the book cover to cover (!) we recognize how busy people are. Thus for those who want to read selectively we provide at the start of each chapter a brief summary of what the chapter is about.

Each chapter has a similar organization. The ways in which the specific needs impact upon behaviour are explored. General principles/ strategies for meeting the needs are identified. Then a 'tips and hints' section offers more specific ideas for implementing these principles/ strategies.

CHAPTER 3

Maintaining a Safe Environment

What this chapter is about

Some of the behaviours that we define as challenging are dangerous in the sense that they threaten physical harm. This may be direct harm to the person himself from self-injurious behaviours such as striking the head against solid surfaces. It may be indirect danger from behaviours such as running off when the person has no safety awareness, sitting down in the middle of busy roads, or eating things that may be poisonous or cause internal obstruction. It may be harm to others – direct forms of aggression such as biting, kicking, hitting, using weapons. It may be the more indirect danger that follows from behaviours such as throwing heavy objects.

Not all behaviours defined as challenging are dangerous. Not all potentially dangerous behaviours will be regarded as challenging (for example sports such as horse riding or rock climbing). There are also forms of danger which are not as obvious as the examples above. Verbal abuse (sexualized language, threats to harm) can be very harmful emotionally although it leaves no physical marks. Some behaviours (coffee drinking, for example) whilst relatively harmless in and of themselves, can be harmful in the long term when carried out to excess. This chapter focuses mainly upon those behaviours that lead to or are very likely to lead to serious physical damage – either to the person or to others. There will be a shorter section at the end focusing upon verbal abuse. The more excessive behaviours which carry a longer term risk are covered in other chapters of the book. This chapter will examine the specific challenges raised by dangerous incidents and how we can address these in a constructive and competent manner.

The issues

Dangerous behaviours can create a great deal of concern in those who live and work with the individual and sometimes in the person himself. They can also create tremendous conflicts around the individual. People may be anxious about intervening to stop the behaviour, particularly if this involves physical intervention, in case they are accused of assault or abuse. Sometimes people are anxious about intervening to stop the behaviour, in case they themselves get hurt or injured. Some people may feel, quite mistakenly, that all 'bad' behaviours should be ignored – yet they find it impossible to do nothing when a person is smashing his head against a wall or when they find themselves or others being pulled across the floor by the hair.

Such anxieties and uncertainties, whilst not unreasonable, are quite likely to make matters worse. The person whose behaviour is causing concern will sense these feelings and may become even more distressed, so the behaviour escalates. If such uncertainties are not resolved it is quite likely that over time varied and inconsistent responses to the behaviour will develop. This will be unhelpful to the person and may result in an increase in anxiety or agitation.

Important principles

We all have a right to be safe and free from inflicted harm. In some countries this may have specific legal backing as in Health and Safety at Work legislation. In our dealings with others, certainly in human service settings, there is a general duty of care by which we are required to do the best that we can to support the rights of those in our care to be safe. This duty may extend quite widely to include colleagues at work and the general public with whom we come into contact during the course of our work. The duty of care is particularly important in our relations with those who are vulnerable and are not in a good position to look after their own interests. Therefore in working with those who behave in dangerous ways on a repeated basis we are required to do the best that we can do in the circumstances to reduce the likelihood of harm both to the person himself and to all others at risk.

When responding to dangerous behaviour there may be a conflict between a 'psychological' response (one intended to make the behaviour less likely to happen in the future) and a health and safety response (one intended to restore safety). In these circumstances the health and safety response always takes priority and we have to find other ways of effecting change in the behaviour.

> *Mary would bang her head on the floor whenever she wanted or needed attention. The banging would get very hard and intense if she was ignored. Her mother knew that when she responded by holding Mary this reinforced the behaviour and so made it more likely that the behaviour would occur again when similar circumstances arose. Should she have ignored Mary until she stopped banging? Of course not! She could not risk her daughter inflicting considerable and permanent damage to herself.*

> *Whenever he wanted space and to be by himself Peter would hit out at other users of his service. Those supporting Peter knew that removing other service users from the vicinity or taking Peter to a quiet room on his own would reinforce the behaviours and make it more likely that Peter would do the same again. Should they have ignored the behaviours until the aggression stopped? Of course not! They could not risk injury to the other service users.*

When supporting a person who shows dangerous behaviour, it is important to organize a response to the behaviour which will contain or limit the dangerous incident. This work will need to take place before getting down to a more detailed assessment of the factors contributing to its occurrence and to planning interventions aimed at reducing the behaviour in the longer term. If people feel frightened, uncertain and unconfident, it is unlikely that real progress can be made until those feelings are dealt with. It is important, therefore, to be able to respond to dangerous situations rapidly, clearly (knowing what one is trying to do) and confidently. It is also important that the response to the behaviour is predictable to the person in a given set of circumstances. It is therefore a key element in supporting those who act in dangerous ways to have an agreed plan for responding to dangerous incidents. Such plans are sometimes called reactive strategies, emergency drills or behaviour management programmes. The main aim of such a plan is to reduce the likelihood of harm to all those involved. It is also a means of building the confidence of those who support the person.

The key skill involved in keeping people safe and free from inflicted harm is risk analysis. Risk analysis involves judgements about probabilities not certainties – the probability of the behaviour occurring; the probability of responding to it effectively and safely. Risk is a function of three interlinking factors:

- The behaviour itself

- The circumstances in which it occurs

- The resources available for managing the situation.

A competent analysis of these factors will enable us to act in ways that reduce the likelihood of harm to all those involved. It cannot guarantee that no harm will occur, it can only reduce the likelihood of harm occurring.

Strategies for maintaining a safe environment

Dangerous incidents are often linked to level of arousal. Arousal involves the adrenaline (heart rate, muscle tension, sweat glands) and behavioural systems. All individuals have an optimal, comfortable level of arousal although people vary in absolute terms as to where this level is. Whilst operating at this level people function at their best, managing a whole range of day-to-day pressures. When arousal levels shift in an upward or downward direction, this leads to changes in behaviour. Such changes will often be clearly evident during the build up and aftermath of a behavioural incident when arousal level and the behaviours which are linked to it may pass through a number of distinct stages. Whilst not all behavioural incidents conform to this pattern, many do and the model generated by this pattern is relevant to the practical management of all incidents. This model is described in Figure 3.1.

Baseline	Person functioning at optimal level
Stage 1.	Something pleasant, frightening or aversive happens and this triggers an increase in arousal. The person may become anxious or angry or excited.
Stage 2.	Arousal continues to build. It may build rapidly (over a few seconds) or very slowly (over minutes or hours, even days), depending upon the trigger, the presence of additional triggering events and individual differences in 'arousability'. The person may become irritable, demanding, threatening or abusive, less able to cope with everyday demands.
Stage 3.	Arousal peaks and the person loses control. The person may become aggressive, destructive or self injurious.
Stage 4.	Arousal levels start to drop and the person begins to calm. However, further stressors whilst arousal is still fairly high may cause rapid increases in arousal and further incidents as arousal peaks again.
Stage 5.	Arousal drops sharply, sometimes falling below the individual's comfortable level, causing the person to become sleepy, tired or miserable for a while.
Baseline	Arousal returns to the optimal comfort level.

Figure 3.1 A model of arousal and behaviour

The model describes five stages in the build up and aftermath of a dangerous incident. Action may be required at any or all of the five stages in order to maintain safety – by preventing unnecessary incidents and managing safely those incidents which do occur. Before moving on to a discussion of these strategies, however, it is important to note that the first step in this work always involves a clear definition of the behaviour of concern. Strategies must be built around a *specific* behaviour (pulling other people's hair, hitting head to solid surface, threatening with a knife) not a *general* type of behaviour (aggression, self injury) and not a fuzzy concept (tantrum, disturbed). People interpret situations differently, they respond according to their interpretations and perceptions. Given the importance of speed and consistency it is vital to make crystal clear which behaviour the strategy is for.

Preventing incidents

GENERAL PRINCIPLES

Prevention of incidents involves taking steps to reduce immediately the number of incidents that occur. These will include removal of unwanted stressors and engineering situations so that arousal levels are kept at a steady and comfortable level. Strategies might include:

- Reorganizing the environment to make it less stressful to the individual (smaller groups, decreased noise level, providing a safe area to which the person can withdraw when she becomes anxious or overwhelmed).

- Reorganizing activities in which the person is asked to participate, in order to decrease exposure to stressful, aversive activities which are not necessary for the person's overall well being.

- Rescheduling the people who work with the individual, so that only favoured people provide the needed support.

- Removing unnecessary triggers which might lead to conflict (for example, not putting the pepper pot on the table when you know that throughout the meal the person will keep trying to pour its entire contents over his food, that you will be intervening to stop this and your action will be causing increasing agitation in him).

Those supporting the person may resist these kinds of basic preventative strategies. For example, teachers may feel under pressure to adhere to the teaching curriculum at all times; altering the environment may be felt to intrude upon the rights of others who use that particular service; scheduling only preferred people to support the individual may violate written (or unwritten) service policies. Not least, people paid to support may in general resist changes to their own preferred habits and routines. Yet careful consideration of situations where problems arise may reveal that when there are high levels of agitation and there is a high risk of incidents the curriculum does not get delivered anyway, the rights of others get much more seriously violated, routines get disrupted and preferred people are relied upon to deal with the situation anyway. Of course none of these strategies are long-term solutions. Such solutions take time (as the rest of this book will illustrate). In the meantime it may be important to reduce stress and danger as much as is possible. Unless we do this it is quite unlikely that the longer-term work will ever get undertaken.

TIPS AND HINTS

(1) A quick and easy way to identify unwanted stressors is to list out all the circumstances in which the behaviour is most likely to occur. Add to this list by imagining that you were given unlimited resources to create 'a day from hell' for the person – a day in which the behaviour in question would be very likely to occur frequently and intensely. What would be the key elements of such a day? Answers to this question will generate a number of ideas about things that could be done which could reduce the likelihood of the behaviour occurring, by removing unnecessary triggers.

(2) A quick and easy way to identify situations in which the likelihood of the behaviour is minimized is to list out the circumstances in which the behaviour is least likely to occur. Add to this list by imagining that you have unlimited resources to create a 'day in heaven' for the person – a day in which the behaviour in question would be very unlikely to occur. What would be the key elements of such a day? Answers to this question may generate a number of ideas about positive actions which could be taken to maintain optimal levels of arousal.

(3) Have a transition ritual that is gone through after one activity is completed and before the next one begins (for example some breathing exercises, physical exercises, a particular piece of music). This will help to diffuse any emotional build up

created by transition and help to focus on the upcoming activity.

(4) Meal times are often a peak time for behavioural incidents. Consider reducing the noise level and waiting times. Look to enhancing food quality and to introducing snacks between meals to reduce craving.

(5) Waiting times commonly predict challenging behaviour – make sure the person always has something available to engage her attention if she is going to have to wait.

(6) Unstructured times also predict behavioural incidents. The more time can be structured the better.

(7) Travel times can be problematic. Use transition cards (photographs, symbols, written reminders) to keep the person oriented to the destination, ensure the availability of engaging activities during the journey.

(8) For a number of people who engage in severe self injury, swimming and floating in water can be an activity when they are freed from the behaviour.

(9) If you are working with someone who injures himself severely it is always easier to fade out the use of physical protective devices (such as splints) than it is to fade out another person continuously holding the individual.

(10) It is a matter of judgement about what preventative measures could be actioned without impinging in a serious way upon the rights and quality of life of the person himself and of others who are involved. Risk analysis is important here – what is the risk if we take this action, what is the risk if we do not.

Defusing conflicts

GENERAL PRINCIPLES

Incidents may occur when the individual wants one thing and those who support her want another. Whilst some conflicts are inevitable, others may be quite unnecessary. Conflicts can trigger an increase in arousal (Figure 3.1, Stage 1). Conflicts easily turn into battles and battles involve winners and losers. In the battle for victory in day-to-day conflicts everyone can become a loser. For example, we may put pressure on the person to complete a task, he refuses to comply and hurts himself. We persist, he hurts others in his efforts to communicate his message to us and the task gets forgotten in the process. We lose because he does not do the activity. The person loses because he is stopped from participating in the day's outing, which he always enjoys.

The skilled management of conflict is about effecting an outcome that is acceptable to both parties, an outcome which ensures that no one loses face, an outcome from which everyone gains something positive.

TIPS AND HINTS

(1) Check out that your requests and prohibitions are valid. Ask yourself 'Whose needs are being met – the individual's or mine; what does the individual gain from going along with my suggestions?' As parents, carers or educators we are not infallible. We are easily drawn into conflicts and battles of will with those in our care.

(2) When setting a limit try to redirect the person to another topic or activity in order to switch the focus of attention.

(3) Make careful use of humour to lighten the mood (but remember that subtle, social humour may be misinterpreted and escalate distress).

(4) Try resolving conflicts by offering a compromise ('You come for the drive and you can sit in the car and watch while the others go horse riding. You won't have to ride').

(5) Always show appreciation of co-operation, including direct incentives ('Tidy your room and then we'll have coffee together').

(6) Communicate clearly what is to happen after the less favoured activity is completed (ideally this should be a more favoured activity).

(7) Give a warning before asking the individual to stop doing one thing and move on to another.

(8) With those for whom it is feasible, try to directly negotiate a compromise with a win-win outcomes (I get what I need from the situation and you also get what you need from the situation). Negotiation involves

- Assertively informing the person what it is that needs to be done

- Listening to and acknowledging her objections

- Explaining why this needs to be done

- Offering a compromise ('OK, you wash the cups and I'll do the plates', 'I can see you are not quite ready yet, in 5 minutes then').

Diffusing the build up of arousal in the person

GENERAL PRINCIPLES

For some behaviours there are warning signs that an incident is likely to occur. Usually there is a build up in agitation, arousal or excitement (Figure 3.1, Stage 2). External signs may include an increase in noisiness, an increase in activities such as pacing, hand movements or rocking, a decrease in concentration. The person may become irritable, argumentative or threatening. It is often possible to divert incidents by taking appropriate action at this stage, before an outburst occurs. The earlier in the build up the action to diffuse the arousal is taken the more likely it is to be successful. The nature of the action to be taken depends very much upon knowing the individual and it may be necessary to plan different responses to different levels of the build up.

TIPS AND HINTS

(1) At the early stages of a build up a firm, clear direction to a distracting activity can often help. A complete change of situation can also help.

(2) Acknowledge that the person is feeling uncomfortable.

(3) When trying to reduce arousal avoid use of the words 'no', 'stop', and 'bad' – these may directly trigger rapid increases in arousal.

(4) If the person has learned a self-calming strategy, this might be the time to encourage its use. Strategies such as relaxation, deep breathing or a brisk walk will directly reduce arousal levels. Some kinds of music may facilitate relaxation, as may the informed use of aromatherapy oils.

(5) When the agitation level is high, often the best approach is to offer the person quietness and space. Sometimes reduced lighting may be helpful. Offer a favoured repetitive activity, such as drawing, doing puzzles, tearing paper or twiddling a straw or other comforter. Such repetitive activities are likely to be more effective than trying directly to talk him down or calm him by interacting with him.

(6) Attention to your own body is important. Avoid too much language, sustained eye contact and arm waving. Try not to approach the person too quickly or to stand directly facing him.

Controlling your own arousal

GENERAL PRINCIPLES

When agitation is high and dangerous incidents are anticipated, it is natural for our own arousal to increase. Such an increase in arousal will be accompanied by changes in our behaviour – change in voice pitch, speed of talking, amount of speech; change in body posture and movement. Such changes may increase the arousal of the other person who will also sense directly in us any strong underlying emotions such as anger or fear. It is therefore important for all those who support an individual who engages in dangerous behaviour to be aware of their own feelings and reactions and to learn how to manage them constructively.

TIPS AND HINTS

(1) Learn a physical relaxation skill so that you can calm your bodily arousal (muscle tension, heart rate, sweatiness). At various moments throughout the day think about your bodily tension. Learn to recognize when your body is tense, the particular areas which are most sensitive to tension states (individuals vary). Practise steady breathing for a slow count of 10 breaths, relaxing the tense parts of your body as you breathe out. Practise in the car, whilst standing at the bus stop, whilst doing the washing up – it only takes a few seconds!

(2) Recognize unhelpful thoughts that may go through your mind that may increase your arousal level. Learn to think about situations differently so that they do not seem so personal or deliberate and so that you do not punish yourself with unrealistic expectations of being perfect. Practise these more helpful thoughts. Examples include:

Unhelpful thoughts	Helpful thoughts
It's personal against me	It's not personal, he does it with everyone
She's trying to upset me	She has no idea how this really affects me
She's doing it deliberately	She's only trying to get her needs met
I'm hopeless – I can't control the situation	I can only do my best
Everyone's watching me to see how I handle this	People are watching out for my safety

(3) Recognize which aspects of your body language change when you become anxious (ask colleagues to bring these to your attention) and practise controlling these.

Reducing the impact of the behaviour

GENERAL PRINCIPLES

There are often practical steps that can be taken that reduce the impact or seriousness of an incident. Our response to dangerous behaviour is likely to be determined by the harm it causes. If the behaviour causes pain or injury to the person or to others our responses are likely to be immediate attempts at rapidly stopping the behaviour. If the impact of the behaviour can be reduced so that harm or pain is avoided or lessened (for example, by wearing a hat to reduce the severity of hair pulling), this may at the very least provide us with extra time to try to work through the situation with the person so that calm is restored without further intervention being necessary. Judgements about the appropriateness of taking these measures may sometimes involve judgements about an individual's rights and quality of life. Risk analysis may be relevant in such situations – what are the relative risks of taking or not taking such precautions.

TIPS AND HINTS

(1) Consider keeping long hair tied back if working with individuals who pull hair.

(2) Do not wear jewellery when working with individuals who are likely to be aggressive. Rings can have sharp edges and cause injury during an incident. Earrings and necklaces or chains can be pulled and cause pain.

(3) Remove sharp knives from the environment if the person is likely to use these as weapons.

(4) Wear long sleeves and trousers if working with someone who bites or pinches.

(5) Consider wearing gloves when working closely with someone who scratches.

(6)   Look at seating arrangements so that the person can easily exit a situation without obstruction during high risk times.

(7)   When supporting someone who bangs his head against hard surfaces, have large cushions available in every room to buffer head-to-surface hitting.

(8)   When working with a person who shows a high frequency of self-injurious behaviour, consider equipping her with protective devices (helmets, splints).

(9)   Get the person who hits out at himself or others to wear clothes with deep pockets so that he can be encouraged to keep his hands in his pockets at high risk times.

Responding to incidents of the behaviour

GENERAL PRINCIPLES

Just as contingency plans need to be made for prevention, so too plans need to be made for responding to the dangerous behaviour itself when it occurs (Figure 3.1, Stage 3). The contents of such reactive strategies or emergency drills will be determined by the nature of the behaviour, the level of risk and the resources usually available for dealing with that behaviour in that situation (for example, people available, space). Although consistency is desirable, safety issues may require different strategies for different situations. The strategy for responding to an incident in a crowded minibus may be different from the strategy in a department store, which in turn may be different from the strategy for responding in the house in the middle of the night. Level of risk and availability of resources are likely to be different across these situations.

Those involved can best devise a drill by going through the following steps:

(1)   Identify all the possible options for responding to the behaviour when it occurs.

(2)   Carry out a risk–benefit analysis for each of these options. The risks and benefits would include physical issues (harm, damage, cost), psychological issues (distress, humiliation, embarrassment, damage to relationships, loss of self esteem)

and legal issues (law of the land, organizational policies) for all those involved.

(3) From this analysis identify the option or, more likely, combination of options that is feasible to implement now and offers the greatest benefits and the least risks.

(4) Identify the additional resources that would add benefits and decrease risks. Such resources might include additional staffing, access to alternative transport, alternative housing or school provision, additional training.

(5) Plan a drill based upon the favoured option, given current resource levels.

(6) Practise the drill. It is vital that drills are role played out to refine the details. This will also increase the likelihood of implementation and decrease the likelihood of injury.

(7) Write up the agreed drill.

(8) Decide how to pursue the acquisition of the resources identified in (4). This is a longer–term strategy for reducing risk but, nevertheless, an important one. If those who have the power to provide resources are not given correct information, then resources will not be deployed effectively. If they are informed of risks – risks assessed in a professional, systematic and objective way – they will be under greater pressure to respond than if our requests come simply as an emotional plea.

(9) Implement the drill.

(10) Review its implementation on a regular basis so that any necessary amendments can be made in a planned way.

Figure 3. 2 summarizes the decision making process. Figure 3.3 offers a model for writing up the management strategy.

(1) When looking at the options for responding to the behaviour always consider the option of doing nothing. Many people with autism find physical contact from others aversive. Their distress may be compounded at times when arousal and agitation are high. Thus a physical intervention may serve to worsen the behaviour and result in a longer calming phase.

(2) When trying to reach a group decision on the drill to respond to the behaviour, after the risk analysis go round the group and ask each person in turn their favoured combination without others questioning or commenting. Only after everyone has spoken try to reach a group decision. This stops the group being dominated by its strongest members and contributes to building the confidence of all.

(3) If physical intervention is judged the best option, seek proper training as soon as possible. There are now available a number of non-aggressive, respectful approaches to physical work of this kind and there is evidence that such training can reduce incidents and the likelihood of injury when incidents do occur.

(4) For those implementing emergency drills, try to develop the mind set that this is part of what we do (like fire drills); it is an area of competence not an admission of failure; the person gains from the confidence of others in dealing with these situations. Such a mind set may help to contain some of the inevitable, strong emotions evoked – fear, anger, guilt, embarrassment.

Managing the end/aftermath of the incident

GENERAL PRINCIPLES

The period immediately following an incident (Figure 3.1, Stage 4) is a time of high risk for further incidents. In addition, the aftermath of an incident, too, may leave a victim in need of support and a 'perpetrator' who remains emotionally fragile from, for example, being physically held or being out of control (Figure 3.1, Stage 5). Sensitive manage-

ment of these stages is as important, therefore, as the management of
the earlier stages and should be carefully planned.

TIPS AND HINTS

(1) Plan how to respond to the person whose behaviour gave rise
to concern once the incident is over. He may need to use the
toilet, have a drink or a wash, lie down for a while, spend
time on his own.

(2) Asking the person to apologize or to make restitution too
early after the incident may escalate the situation again. The
same applies to giving an explanation to the person about the
effect of her behaviour and an explanation about what should
have happened instead. Wait until she has completely
recovered if you feel that apologies, restitution or
explanations are important.

(3) If another person has been injured, hurt or frightened, he
may need time away from the individual (minutes, hours or
even days – depending upon the severity of the incident).

(4) The victim of an assault may need time to talk about the
incident. He may need reassurance that he acted appropriately
and that his upset is natural and acceptable.

(5) Those involved in the management of the incident may need
to discuss what happened – to check that agreed procedures
were followed, to identify if it proved impossible to follow
the agreed procedures and to learn any lessons from the
management of the incident that would be helpful for the
management of future incidents.

(6) Once the person has calmed and recovered and any apologies
and explanations have been given, there should be no further
mention of the incident and he should be supported to return
to his activities. If a discussion with the individual about his
behaviour is thought to be important this should be part of
an ongoing, structured, supportive relationship that does not
involve blame or reprimand (why did you do that then) but is
about a partnership to learn.

Maintaining a Safe Environment

(1) Specify the behaviour of concern

(2) Identify those who need to be involved in the decision making

(3) Identify the mechanisms for decision making

(4) Draw up a plan – plan elements to include

- Activities to prevent incidents

- Approaches to conflict management

- Approaches to diffusing arousal

- Activities to reduce the impact of the behaviour

- Response to incidents based upon

  - Identification of the response options

  - Risk–benefit analysis of options identified

  - Identification of the response which is feasible, maximizes benefits, minimizes risks

  - Practice of response drill

(5) Write up the plan

(6) Implement and review plan

(7) Pursue additional resources identified as relevant by the planning process

Figure 3.2 Maintaining a safe environment – the decision making process

THIS IS A CRITICAL INCIDENT SUPPORT PLAN
For:
Drawn up on:

PLAN BACKGROUND

The specific behaviour of concern is

Those involved in drawing up the plan are

Those who have seen the plan and agree to it are

Those who have seen the plan and disagree with it are

The things that are being done to find out why the behaviour occurs
are

Figure 3.3 Critical Incident Support Plan Format

PLAN DETAILS

The things that we will do to prevent incidents

    (1)   Changes in environment, activities, routines, supports

    (2)   Management of known triggers

    (3)   Ways of working when there is a conflict

    (4)   Ways of working to reduce identified increases in arousal

The things that we will do to reduce the impact of incidents

The ways that we will respond to incidents

	What the individual does	What we will do
First signs		
Build up		
Final level		

Figure 3.3 continued

The ways that we will manage the aftermath of the incident

(1) How we will work with the individual

(2) How we will work with the others affected by the
     incident

The way that we will evaluate the plan's effectiveness
Review system details

CRITICAL INCIDENT SUPPORT PLAN REVIEW SHEET

Date	People Involved	Outcome of review

Figure 3.3 continued

Managing verbal abuse

GENERAL PRINCIPLES

Some people with autism may show verbally abusive behaviour. Verbal abuse takes a number of forms – threats to harm, sexualized language, racist or other discriminatory forms of abuse. Verbal abuse can be very damaging to those on the receiving end, leaving them feeling helpless, angry and violated in the most intimate of ways. It can have a major impact upon morale. Yet it leaves no visible mark and does not generate in observers the same urgent concern as physical assault. It is our experience that the strength of emotion generated by this particular behaviour can easily result in carers forgetting that people with autism have great difficulties in social understanding – they attribute to such behaviours intentionality, insight and the deliberate infliction of distress. Such attributions, combined with the strong emotions, can lead to very unprofessional responses. It is therefore essential that the seriousness of this behaviour is recognized and we would urge that a response to verbal abuse be devised following the guidelines described in this chapter for responding to physically dangerous behaviours. This will help to indicate how seriously the behaviour is taken and will also generate a consistent response to the individual.

TIPS AND HINTS

(1) Ensure that 'house rules' include reference to the unacceptability of abusive language.

(2) Prepare a verbal and behavioural 'script' which can be consistently used by everyone. This will help to empower those involved, rather than them having to listen powerlessly to what is being said. It will help those involved to remain detached.

(3) It is important for those supporting staff or family members dealing with this situation to be aware of the possible impact of verbal abuse. People will need the chance to talk about the feelings that the behaviour generates.

(4) It may be necessary to take practical action and limit people's exposure to the behaviour by planning systematically who works with the person and for how long (the family equivalent would be using other family members or providing home support to give them a break for a time).

(5) Sometimes it may be necessary to allow someone who is a consistent target of verbal abuse the choice of not working with the person for an extended period of time; or to provide families with more extended holiday or relief care.

As with all other behaviours, the long term solution lies in analyzing what the behaviour is about and working through the sorts of approaches described in the rest of this book. The main point from a health and safety perspective is that verbal behaviour of this kind should be taken very seriously indeed.

Concluding remarks

Most of this book is about how we can understand better the needs of people who have autism labels and whose behaviour is cause for concern. It is about positive, everyday things that we can do to help them move on in their lives. If a person has been engaging in a behaviour for a long time it is a sure bet that he will continue to do so and that change will take time. It is therefore vital to acknowledge that whilst we are developing insights and positive support, problematic behaviours will continue. If the behaviour is clearly dangerous this means there is a need to develop competent responses to these incidents, responses which respect the right to safety of the person himself and those who live with, work with and otherwise encounter the person. This is a difficult and controversial area but one that needs to be addressed honestly and respectfully. We believe that there are relatively straightforward things that can be done to develop good practice and we have tried to illustrate these in this chapter. We also believe that unless this area is addressed honestly it will not be possible to develop and sustain for people who act in dangerous ways the kinds of work that the rest of this book endorses.

CHAPTER 4

Understanding

What this chapter is about

Many behaviours of concern occur in a context where the person does not know what is required in a situation – her chosen way of dealing with a situation may be socially inappropriate but she may not realize this – or when she does not understand what is happening in a situation. People with autism have many difficulties encoding and understanding information available or presented to them. These difficulties increase as the complexity of the information increases. Such difficulties may be particularly evident at transition points, when familiar routines are broken, when abstract information, such as time-related concepts, are presented or when choices need to be made. Difficulties are compounded when the person's arousal is high or her attention is so taken up with something that she cannot take in important information which is available to her.

Behaviour in these situations will often reflect severe distress and the attempts of the person to make the world safe, to escape uncertainty or other discomforts. Part of this may be extreme assertion, a determination to mould the world to the way she wants it to be, regardless of the social feasibility or acceptability of this. It may also reflect her honest attempts to 'do the right thing' without having the inborn skills to know what the right thing is. These are central areas of difficulty for people with autism. Our focus in this chapter, therefore, is on the difficulties that people with autism have with understanding on a day-to-day basis the world around them and how we might support them to make the outside world less confusing and more easily understandable.

Links between behaviour and difficulties in understanding

There are several different ways in which understanding may directly influence behaviour (see Chapter 1). There can be secondary effects also upon the person's thoughts and feelings when they grow up 'getting things wrong' a lot of the time and to these we will also give some consideration.

Problems in decoding verbal language

Many people who attract autism labels have difficulties extracting meaning from spoken language. For some this will mean a complete inability to get meaning from verbal language. For others there may be understanding of language but the person experiences problems getting information in the correct sequence. There may be difficulties with abstract concepts and idioms. The person may have difficulties 'reading between the lines' or understanding unspoken messages – he takes what is said literally. Sometimes the system works very slowly – the person grasps things only a little at a time: if too much language occurs too quickly he is overwhelmed. The outcome of such difficulties can be that the person acts inappropriately – innocently doing the wrong thing in a situation. The outcome can also include powerful emotions – fear because the person does not know of a situation until it occurs, distress as she loses information coming in to the system too quickly, confusion or panic as she misinterprets the message. Behaviours that result may be part of the powerful emotional reaction to this situation.

Problems in reading social signs

Many people experience significant problems around interaction with other people. At one level the person may be quite uninterested in other people, paying little or no attention to them except perhaps when they can help meet an immediate need or as sources of sensory pleasure. Even if there is interest, he may not know how to behave around people. He may not share others' priorities and agendas. He may not pick up on social and emotional cues from others that would help him adjust his behaviour to the situation. He may have difficulty distinguishing fact from fiction – understanding that something is a joke, understanding that what he sees on television may not be real.

As a result of such difficulties the person may avoid or escape from contact with others, finding the attention of others intrusive. He may resist going along with other people's requests because he does not see the importance of what is being asked of him (for example, preferring to shred clothes rather than do the ironing or practise writing). Behaviour around other people may be socially inappropriate (for example, poking someone in the eyes in order to enjoy the sight of tears glistening on the face) or clumsy (addressing others at length about his own favourite topic unaware that the listener may be bored or uninterested).

Managing multiple channels of information

There may be a range of difficulties which arise from a difficulty in simultaneously processing information from a number of sources. The person may focus too narrowly on one particular input to the exclusion of all other information. For example, he may lock into the ray of sunlight on the carpet and exclude all other information – other people talking or moving, the door opening. He may have difficulty integrating information involving a number of different inputs (for example, tone of voice, words, gestures and facial expression, context) to extract meaning from a situation. Linked to these difficulties may be problems with switching focus from one topic or activity to another.

The effects of difficulties with managing multiple channels of information may be significant. If the person focuses too tightly on a single input, he may be surprised or upset because changes or transitions seem to occur without apparent warning; he may feel threatened or anxious as he becomes suddenly aware that others are talking, looking or standing very close. Problems with integrating information from several sources may make it hard for him to extract meaning from group situations or complex social encounters. Difficulties with switching focus may mean he gets stuck with a particular movement, topic or task, feeling increasingly out of control and unable to stop until someone else intervenes to move him on.

Difficulties with problem solving

There are people who appear to be tied exclusively to personal and immediate experiences. They find it hard to conceive of possibilities, to imagine things. Thus they may find it hard to put themselves in someone else's shoes, to solve problems when things don't go according to plan, to think ahead and plan into the future, to make choices. Such difficulties may result in extreme distress when things do not go according to plan or when things go wrong – the person cannot solve the problem or put another plan into action. Difficulties with solving problems and thinking ahead may mean the person persists with a particular way of doing things, over and over, rather than trying new possibilities; it may mean he resorts to behaviours which others define as obsessions, rituals or stereotypies when problems arise – just because they are familiar.

Difficulties with the sense of time

A number of people appear to experience difficulty with judgements about time – judging time lapse (sensing the difference between 'in half an hour' and 'next week'; grasping what is meant by 'soon', 'later', 'tomorrow'). Likewise there may be difficulties with the sense of time passing – memories for events remote in time may be as vivid as those for recent events. Some people seem to inhabit a 'simultaneous universe' of past and present. Experiencing these difficulties means that when the person is told something will happen, he expects it to happen immediately, being unable to grasp that the event *will* take place…but not for some time. He may focus more and more upon it, get more and more wound up and may eventually lose control. Many families and practitioners have adapted to these difficulties by not giving the people they support too much warning about future events, especially about events which are significant.

Other blocks to processing important information

Accessing information from the world around may be difficult enough. These difficulties may be compounded by other more active intrusions. These can block access to important information and may also create distress in their own right. The hypersensitivities to specific sensory stimuli (sounds, light, textures, smells, tastes) may act in this way. High priority items such as personal passions, rituals, worries or compulsions (loosely termed 'obsessions') may dominate processing space, some creating distress in themselves, all making it harder to process important information about what is going on in the world outside. These topics are covered in detail in Chapters 8 and 9 but are mentioned here to highlight their importance in the problems the person may experience with processing day-to-day information.

The effects of growing up with difficulties in understanding

The autobiographical accounts of a small number of individuals illustrate vividly the confusion, uncertainty and anxiety that can be generated by difficulties with understanding and processing day-to-day information. They show how difficult new learning becomes and how hard it is to enjoy life. They speak to the difficulty in achieving a sense of confidence and the growing awareness of being different. Many of those who write their stories have come through this and accept and celebrate those differences. In our work, however, we meet many who do not celebrate their difference. They appear to rage at themselves or at others and they may become depressed about their differences. It also seems likely that another outcome of the experience is to develop rigid rituals and to avoid new experiences so that the world is kept predictable and safe. This brings short-term gains but in the long run limits the quality of life that the individual can experience. We would also speculate that some, as a result of their cumulative experiences, withdraw socially, either for a time or as a more permanent attempt at the resolution of distress (see Chapter 6).

We have outlined a wide range of difficulties in understanding that people with autism labels may experience. Not everyone so identified will have all of these difficulties. We need to build a profile of the particular difficulties that the person experiences currently and identify whether information processing and understanding difficulties play a role in the occurrence of specific behaviours which the person shows (see Appendix 1). It is only by knowing the person and analyzing the specific behaviour of concern that we can tailor our support to the needs of the individual. This is important because what follows is a general overview of support strategies and not everyone identified as autistic needs all these strategies. However strategies that enhance the many different kinds of understandings that make the world a more accessible place will be a major focus of support for many people with the autism label.

Strategies for supporting the person to understand the world

Much of this book is about helping people to understand and interact more successfully in their social world. The strategies covered in this chapter are one aspect of the work. The approaches described here aim to increase the person's understanding of the world. If they are effective it will help to make the world a more predictable place. This in turn will reduce anxiety, enhance well being, encourage the individual to engage more confidently with the social world and, in the long run, make it easier to learn new skills and coping strategies.

When we talk about helping people who have difficulties processing everyday information to make better sense of the world, there are core specific areas that we need to address. In particular, we need to structure and present information in a way that makes it easier for the person to understand

- What…is happening, what is going to happen, what she is supposed to be doing now, what she is going to be doing
- When…the person can and will do something, when he is expected to start, stop or finish what he is doing
- Where…certain behaviours are supposed to occur and where they are not
- Why…things happen as they do.

Before we detail important strategies we would like to acknowledge and pay tribute first to the work of Division TEACCH at the University of North Carolina, Chapel Hill. Their research, practical experience and wisdom accumulated over decades has made an enormous contribution to identifying techniques of support that help to make the world understandable for people regarded as autistic. We would also like to pay tribute to the work of Carol Gray (1994a, 1994b) for the development of social stories and comic strip conversations, a more recent but invaluable addition to helping people make sense of the thoughts and feelings of others and develop effective social functioning. What follows owes much to the contributions of these sources.

Managing the physical environment

GENERAL PRINCIPLES

Visual, auditory, movement and olfactory stimuli may interfere with the ongoing processing of information. It is important, therefore, to give attention to

- Décor – simple patterns, soft colours, plain floor coverings and curtains
- Lighting – soft and uniform
- Clutter – minimizing the number of redundant items
- Noise – eliminating or minimizing unpleasant or unnecessary noise from, for example, sound systems, televisions, chairs scraping on floors, cutlery scraping on hard table surfaces
- Movement – reducing rapid, unpredictable movements.

Keeping the physical environment calm in this way may help the person to focus upon information that is important rather than be distracted by intrusive sensory stimulation.

TIPS AND HINTS

(1) Consider using background sound, such as rhythmic music, to block the intrusion of uncontrollable noises from outside and to help maintain a calm atmosphere. Having a personal stereo can be one way to effect this.

(2) Consider using a background aroma to block the intrusion of uncontrollable smells.

Providing structure and routines

GENERAL PRINCIPLES

There are two key issues here that are often subsumed under the general heading of 'structure'. One is to develop routines. Routines provide predictability and familiarity and are a key element in enabling the person to learn what happens on what day, which activity follows what, the order in which tasks need to be done. Routines also reduce the burden on the problem solving system, a key difficulty for many people.

The second issue is to ensure that the environment operates in a way that keeps the person engaged as much of the time as possible. This is not just about reducing boredom and the problem-solving load. It is also about reducing vulnerability to being overwhelmed by internal experiences that may explode unannounced into consciousness; or to getting stuck in repetitive activities or behaviour from which the individual cannot easily disengage.

TIPS AND HINTS

(1) Provide a structured timetable of daily and weekly activities.

(2) Organize activities so that they follow a regular pattern (including how the activity starts and ends – see earlier mention of 'transition' rituals).

(3) Develop work or activity routines whereby a task is always approached in a specific (rather than random) way – left to right, top to bottom. Place the dirty dishes on the left and stack them clean on the right. Lay the clothes out on the bed from left to right in the order that they will be put on. Start working on the list from the top and work systematically down to the bottom.

(4) Make sure that an individual always has something available that is likely to engage his attention when travelling, standing in line or during other kinds of 'waiting' time.

Managing verbally presented information

GENERAL PRINCIPLES

Most interactions with the person will have a verbal component. It is important that this is managed in a way that is helpful to that person and this may require some adaptation of our own preferred individual style. One element of this is to chunk information and present it at a measured pace. Whatever medium you are working in (speech, sign, pictures, writing), when you want to inform somebody about an event, a change or a choice, focus on the key elements in the message and allow time for the processing of each chunk. The aim is to avoid unnecessary or distracting information and not go too quickly.

The second crucial element is always to present information in a very concrete and specific way. State exactly what will happen, exactly what is wanted. Leave no message unstated. Do not expect the other person to 'read between the lines' or infer anything. Try also to put information in positive format – what the person is going to do, rather than what she not going to do; what is wanted rather than what is not wanted. This reduces the likelihood of misunderstanding rather than being some warm, fuzzy notion of political correctness.

TIPS AND HINTS

(1) Avoid using negative statements when giving information or instructions (see also Chapter 11). A positive statement about what is wanted ('Talk quietly') is far more likely to be understood than a negatively phrased statement ('Don't shout').

(2) Avoid words like 'wait' and 'calm down' (unless the person has been taught a specific behaviour to use in response to these instructions). These words are often used in quite emotionally charged situations but are very abstract – they give the individual no real idea about what they are supposed to do. Be more specific – think about a more helpful positive instruction to use: 'Look at the magazine', 'Fiddle with your key ring', 'Do your breathing exercises', 'Sit down there'.

(3) Avoid words such as 'maybe' or 'later'. These represent extremes of ambiguity. Be more specific: 'I don't know, ask me after lunch' instead of 'Maybe' or 'When you've read three pages of your book' rather than 'Later'.

(4) Pay particular attention to how you give information about activities that the individual will engage in. The information should inform the person exactly what they are to do, how much, when the activity will end and what they will do after that. For example, simply telling him 'We are going to the seaside today' is highly ambiguous – when do we go, how do we get there, what will we do there, when do we come back – if ever? A clearer way to present the information would be 'Today we are driving in the car to the seaside. We will walk on the beach, have a picnic, get back in the car, drive home, have supper.' Of course, this message might need to be broken down and presented slowly, but the elements need to be covered.

(5) Language may need to be very literal and direct. 'Sit down please' rather than 'Would you mind sitting down', 'Go and bring your laundry back to your bedroom' rather than 'Go and find your laundry', 'Let's put the video-tape in the machine, press play and watch the film' rather than 'Let's watch the video'.

(6) Food is a very important element in many people's lives and can produce some very charged confrontations. If you are going to sit in a restaurant, look at a menu and ask for food, say that rather than 'We're going to have lunch'…because if lunch is not there, the disappointment may be intense.

Using non-verbal media to support verbal language when communicating important day-to-day information

GENERAL PRINCIPLES

Many people with autism work better in the visual channel and a number have hearing difficulties. This has been the great contribution of the TEACCH system and, more recently, the social stories work of

Carol Gray (1994b) – to show how to convey visually (through objects of reference, pictures, photographs, icons, written words) important day-to-day information, forthcoming events, behavioural and social expectations. Using a visual medium achieves a number of objectives – visual processing capacities may be superior to verbal processing capacities, visual is more concrete and forces attention to the key message elements, time becomes a physical dimension (left to right, top to bottom), it reduces the need to hold items in memory whilst taking on new items (this may be especially helpful in relation to choices and planning). However, we like to think about using multiple media rather than just visual because some people identified as autistic have severe visual impairments and may need more tactile presentation. We are also intrigued by the possibility of using odour cues as the sense of smell is a much under-recognized source of human understanding and a sense very clearly important to some people.

TIPS AND HINTS

(1) Allocate specific activities to specific environments or areas of a room. Always direct the person to the area where the activity is to take place. If the person then starts a particular activity in a different area or environment they can then be directed back to the allocated area. For example, in the classroom a 'hobbies' area could be made and students allowed to engage in their favourite 'obsessions' only in that area of the room.

(2) Where several activities occur in a single environment, introduce a specific cue to inform the person which activity is about to take place. The cue could be a particular piece of music, an aroma, a specific covering placed on the table, a symbol or picture placed on the wall.

In one group home the dining room was also used for art and literacy activities. There was a lot of confusion amongst the people who lived there, with frequent agitation prior to activities starting. To help them be clearer about which activity to expect, different table coverings were used – one for eating, one for painting, one for literacy work. This made it easier for them to predict what was going to happen and agitation reduced. In another group home where people had marked visual impairments, aromatherapy oil burners were used to signal forthcoming activities.

(3) Use pictures, symbols, written words, colours, photographs (whichever is most appropriate to the person's level of understanding) to inform her what she will be doing. Draw attention to these systems during communication and have her interact with this system (for example, remove pictures of completed activities, check off tasks completed). If she has difficulty with transitions, make routine use of transition cards to focus attention when moving from one place to the next. The cue must be visible during the transition, either displayed for her or carried by her.

Barry had very limited understanding of language and did not associate pictures or symbols with activities. Whenever a trip was suggested (in the car, on the bus, walking) Barry became upset – he appeared not to understand where he was going. The problem was resolved by providing Barry with different coloured rucksacks that were associated with different activities. Barry learned successfully to associate specific activities with the different colours of the rucksacks used.

Martin's understanding of spoken language was limited but he understood enough to know what activity he was going to when he got into the minibus. Problems arose, however, when the minibus used a different route or stopped off on the way. Martin would become distressed and bang his head. A plastic pocket was attached to the back of the seat in front of his. A photograph of the place or activity to which he was going was put into the pocket. During the journey and whenever Martin showed signs of distress his attention was drawn to the photograph and this worked to relieve his anxieties.

Martha had fluent language and excellent reading skills. She would become very anxious when going out of her home, into the community. She was given a checklist just before each trip. It described the aims of the trip (for example, to buy bread) and the specific details of the visit (for example, walk to the local bakery, choose a loaf, pay for it, walk back home). Martha carried this with her and referred to it whenever she became anxious, to excellent effect.

(4) Use visual or other sensory cues to help the person understand start and end points of activities.

Rita lived in a group home and loved to clear tables after meals. However, her definition of 'meal over' was when she had finished and this proved upsetting to the people she lived with who might still be eating – their plates would be taken, cutlery taken from their hands mid-mouthful! Two cards were made. A red card was used to mean that Rita should stay seated at the table. It was placed on the mantelpiece at the start of the meal. When everyone had finished eating, the red card was removed, a green card was put in its place to signal to Rita that she could clear the tables.

When travelling by car or minibus, Jason would become anxious whenever the vehicle stopped (at junctions, traffic lights, rail crossings). He would try to get out of the vehicle and became distressed when prevented by those supporting him from doing this. A 'seatbelts on' sign was made and clearly displayed in the vehicle as Jason and others took their seats. It was made clear that everyone should stay in their seats until the sign was removed. Using this cue and rule, those working for Jason were able to refocus him from trying to get off the bus whenever it stopped. Whilst it took time to get the rule established it proved very successful in enabling Jason to travel safely and eliminated the confrontations that had been occurring.

(5) You can sometimes prepare individuals for rare but important events with the aid of visually presented information.

Kevin always reacted very badly to any change in his routine. He would become distressed, self-injurious and aggressive. He was due for a hospital overnight admission for tests, which would mean that he would need to be at the hospital very early on the day and go without breakfast or any food or drinks for several hours. One option would have been to give him no warning but this almost certainly would have led to disaster. As an alternative, a week before the admission staff took him, on one of his regular trips into the community, to the hospital and took him up onto the ward, introducing him to some of the staff and showing him around the ward. They took photographs as they went along. They then prepared a story for him, using written words, photographs and illustrations to explain exactly what was going to happen over the two days when Kevin went to hospital. They read the story with him twice each day during that week. On the day itself, his carer announced, 'Kevin today we're going to the hospital. Let's read your story about going to the hospital one more time'. Kevin took the storybook, closed it and handed it back to the carer. He was clearly ready for the event and accepted the changed routine of the two days without question and without any apparent anxiety or distress.

(6) Make available important background information about what is going on in the person's world. Presenting that information visually may enable the person to retain the information better, to check easily and independently if they have forgotten or are uncertain. For example, always post the day's menu on the kitchen notice board (written or photographic).

Louise always needed to know which staff were on shift, who was on holiday and who was off sick. It would cause her severe anxiety if she did not have this information. In response to this anxiety the staff team had photographs taken of themselves. At the start of each shift, the photographs of all those on shift were displayed in the hall. A box (the holiday box) alongside contained the photographs of all staff who were currently 'on holiday' and another box (the 'off sick' box) contained the photographs of any staff who were currently off sick. This enabled Louise to check the board and the boxes as often as she needed in order to reassure herself about the whereabouts of her carers.

(7) Use visual support to help the person understand limits that are placed upon behaviour. For example if it has been decided to allow a question to be asked only twice, to allow only a certain number of drinks of tea during the morning, to allow only a certain amount of juice at breakfast, visual cues can be used not only to help the person understand the limits but to help her keep track. Thus, one can provide a jug of juice with the meal, with the person retaining control of it, but when it

is finished the jug is taken away until the next meal, when another full jug is provided; the person can be provided with a pre-agreed number of 'tea' cards each day, which they can exchange for cups of tea. Once they have no more cards they must wait until the tea cards are handed out again the following day.

Providing early and continuing experience of choice and planning

GENERAL PRINCIPLES

Verbal and non-verbal information systems should be used to teach about choice and planning in a manageable way. Choices can be presented concretely and simultaneously. Choices made can also be the opportunity for stimulating thinking about what is needed to make a choice happen (for example, how to organize a chosen trip or activity). Many behavioural challenges reflect a struggle to control the world – choosing and planning are socially accepted alternatives to achieving that goal.

TIPS AND HINTS

(1) Rather than using open questions ('What would you like to…eat, wear, do, etc.') offer concrete choices between alternatives ('Would you like x or y?')

(2) Create as many opportunities as possible in the person's day to make choices (clothes, food, activities).

(3) Use real objects, photographs or symbols to back up questions about choices. Show together the alternatives which are available.

Communicating clearly about time and time-related concepts

GENERAL PRINCIPLES

Many people with autism labels fail to comprehend concepts of time, timing and related concepts, such as changes, delays, cancellations, when these are presented to them verbally. They may also have a more general difficulty in terms of understanding themselves as a person moving through time, which means a future as well as a past. Yet when these concepts are made more concrete, particularly through the use of visual supports, time becomes accessible as a physical dimension – something that moves, something that disappears. This makes it meaningful for many people who would otherwise struggle with these concepts.

TIPS AND HINTS

(1) The time spans that individuals comprehend will clearly vary. In general it is best to avoid presenting information that projects too far into the future – to err on the side of short.

(2) For those who like to or can cope with information given a longer way ahead, use visually uncluttered calendars or diaries (1 week to 2 pages) to help the person count down towards important events. Get him to cross off days, if he is counting down to an important event. Makeshift 'countdown calendars' can be made using sheets of paper and sticky tape. The important thing is that he is prompted and encouraged to check the calendar daily and cross or tear off the days one by one.

(3) Provide the person with their own visual timetable of activities – weekly, daily or just for the morning/afternoon – whatever the appropriate time span for her. The timetable can be colour coded to help her to discriminate weekdays from weekends (the same colour-coding can be used on the calendar). The timetable can be pictorial, photographic, symbolic, written – even objects of reference can be used to make up such a timetable – depending on what is most appropriate for the individual concerned. Encourage her to 'interact' with the timetable – cross off completed activities, remove completed activities from the timetable into a 'finished' box or envelope.

(4) Where information about a specific activity cannot be provided too far in advance, for fear of the person becoming overexcited or anxious, use 'surprise' or 'mystery' cards which

can be substituted by the actual activity card at the appropriate moment.

(5) Use the calendar or timetable to explain cancellations, delays or changes. Show the person how the schedule or timetable changes by altering the sequence. Remove the card or symbol of the cancelled activity in front of him and show him the activity that is replacing it – place this on the schedule. Even better if you can offer a choice for the substitute activity, to reinforce the sense of control.

Robert had his own diary and would enter all forthcoming activities in the diary – filling it in as far in advance as possible. No one else paid close attention to the diary – it was considered to be Robert's own personal possession. When Robert became depressed some months after moving into a new home, showing a high level of self injury and destructiveness, those working for him realized the importance of his diary. It transpired that a lot of information that Robert had entered was, on the day, incorrect – activities were often cancelled, postponed or changed. Staff began regular, brief daily meetings with Robert to check his diary – if events for the following day were cancelled they would cross out the entry and write in its place what he would be doing instead. They learned that as long as something was written in his diary, Robert believed it would happen (it was no good just telling him that an activity had been cancelled). He did not mind the cancellation itself so long as the correct information was entered in the diary.

(6) Use individual work schedules – visually presented. Visually segment the activity into chunks. Get the person to tick or cross off or remove the information about each chunk, as it is completed so that he can always see what has already been done and how much is left to do.

(7) Adapt clock faces to make them easier to read. Remove second and minute hands, paint the hour hand in a bright colour, place pictures or symbols of fixed activities (for example, drinks time, lunch time, home time) around the clock so that the person can see the hour hand approach and gets some sense of passing time. Use hour glasses and kitchen

timers to help her 'see' the passing of time or know when an activity ends.

Janine lived in a residential home. She appeared unhappy and with-drawn. She constantly talked about wanting to visit her parents – she visited them every two weeks. She would demand the next activity or series of activities (dinner, bath, bed), even before the last had finished. It was as if she believed that by rushing through all her daily activities and repeating the sequence several times over, she might get to go home sooner. All interactions with Janine tended to be negative 'No, Janine, it's not time yet...' Her reaction was to bite the person who said this or to withdraw under a blanket into the corner of the room. Janine was provided with a two-week 'calendar' (14 squares of paper stuck in a line onto a board). The thirteenth and fourteenth squares had a picture of 'home' drawn on them. She was provided also with a daily timetable, which was placed on her bedroom wall, each activity stuck on with sticky tape to a board. A large clock was made up, which had only the hour hand on it. Pictures of fixed activities which occurred during the day and which she had also on her timetable, were fixed around the clock. As each activity was completed she removed the symbol from her timetable. Each morning she tore off another square from her calendar and counted the days she had left before her next visit to her parents. Real time was kept in check by letting her see on the clock that certain activities on her timetable could not occur until the hour hand was pointing directly at the picture that matched the one on her timetable. This intervention allowed Janine to see the passage of time visually (movement of hour hand on clock / removal of completed activities on her timetable / removal of another day from her calendar). It reduced immediately confrontations with her carers. Now, instead of telling her 'No, it's not time yet' they were able to direct her to her calendar, timetable and clock. Within a few weeks she had understood these complex concepts and her anxiety and low mood started to lift.

(8) Develop ongoing life story books. These may help people to understand their own progress across time. A personal archive which includes photographs, text, memorabilia, video diaries, even graphs (for example of height and weight) may help

organize the past and also assist in grasping the concept of 'future', a topic that can cause extreme distress for some people with autism.

(9)   Help the individual monitor his own behaviour in time. Actions can be monitored through verbal discussions ('What did you do in the last five minutes?'), visual analysis ('Which pictures show what you were doing in the last five minutes?'), verbal or visual checklists ('Which things did you do this morning?') and diaries.

Explore ways of explaining why things have happened or do happen

GENERAL PRINCIPLES

In the course of ordinary everyday interactions we need to draw attention to our facial expressions and what they mean and link this to events. We need to spell out what we might be thinking that might influence our upcoming behaviour (for example, something that we might need to do next means we need to stop the ongoing conversation). When offering explanations about events we need to be aware that spoken words, the most favoured medium for 'explanations', may be the least effective way of explaining complex concepts, particularly if they refer to others' thoughts and feelings. Whilst this is a very difficult area there may be alternatives to try. Thus we could try depicting events and social interactions that have occurred using simple line drawings, with speech bubbles to show what has been said and thought bubbles to show what people may have been thinking, as in the technique described as 'comic strip conversations' by Carol Gray (1994a) (see Chapter 7). Another option is to write an account of the event for those who are able to read as this may be far clearer than a spoken account and is easier to go over repeatedly.

TIPS AND HINTS

(1)   If the person enjoys communicating using pictures and stories or letters, then encourage them to use the same when they are trying to get important information over to others.

(2) Introduce the person to talking routinely with the aid of pictures. Talk initially about non-threatening and positive events before moving on to more difficult subjects.

(3) Use stories or fact sheets to explain why particular events occur (for example, why a balanced diet is important, why it rains, why students need to listen to their teacher in class) or why particular things are important to do (for example, why it is important to brush one's teeth, wear a seat belt, visit the dentist, have one's hair cut...). Chapter 7 provides more information on this kind of work.

Concluding remarks

In this chapter we have described a number of strategies which can be used to make the world easier for the person with autism to understand. Such strategies are essentially about making information simpler and clearer – making it *accessible*. This will often mean using media other than just language for giving that information – writing, pictures, cartoons, symbols, colours, music, odours. It may mean providing the person with additional cues to help him understand what, when, where or why things do or will happen. It may mean finding creative ways to help him understand complex concepts such as time. It may mean using environments more creatively to provide greater clarity. Many of the strategies we have described have been demonstrated over many years to be effective in making information easier to understand. Once confusion and misunderstanding is reduced, then anxiety and distress are greatly alleviated; and behaviours which may cause concern reduce. However, there is more than just the impacts upon current behaviours. It would be our contention that if we can make available from as early as possible in life the kinds of supports outlined in this chapter, we will make a significant contribution to the longer-term development of those vital psychological resources, referred to variously as self-efficacy, self-confidence, self-esteem. That is surely the greater prize.

CHAPTER 5

Social Relating

What this chapter is about

This chapter looks at the links between behavioural challenges and the ability to relate to and connect with other human beings. In particular it examines the issues for two groups of people – those who are very withdrawn and socially isolated; and at the other extreme those whose social behaviour is so intrusive that they end up being socially isolated because of rejection or avoidance by others. Being part of a social system usually requires the individual to play an active role in establishing and maintaining relationships and for the social system to reciprocate in a like manner. When things go wrong with the relationships in a person's world, this can have a devastating effect on his or her well being – both physical and psychological. This chapter looks at how behavioural functioning can be improved by building or rebuilding constructive social support and engagement.

Two routes to social isolation

For some people with autism behavioural challenges occur in a context of generalized social isolation and withdrawal. They may:

(1) Spend a lot of time on their own.

(2) Only rarely initiate contact and communication with others.

(3) Withdraw from social contact initiated by others.

(4) Become anxious in the presence of people.

(5) Find it hard to co-operate with requests from others,
     becoming upset when others try to interrupt or disturb what
     they are doing.

For some people this is a long-term way of being in the world. For
others it is a phase, sometimes associated with a generalized loss of well
being. It represents a change from a time when the person was more
engaged socially, more accepting of being around other people and of
co-operating with them. The topic of well being is covered in Chapter 6
which needs to be read in conjunction with this chapter.

   For other people with autism, behavioural challenges occur in the
context not of generalized social isolation and withdrawal, but of
intrusive and inappropriate or disturbing social interactions. They may
fail to respond to social cues to give others physical or mental space.
They may

(1) Be constantly demanding of others' time and attention.

(2) Want to be continuously with an individual for whom they
     have developed a liking, to the point that it becomes
     domineering and intrusive. They may respond negatively
     whenever a person they like spends time with others.

(3) Become skilled at, and apparently take pleasure from, getting
     a 'reaction' from people by acting in negative ways towards
     them. They may develop ways which are specific to different
     individuals and their particular 'weak spots'.

Both extreme withdrawal and extreme intrusion are hard for others to
cope with. People generally find it hard to relate to a person who
constantly rejects them. They find it equally hard to relate to a person
who is overintrusive, or who appears selfish or lacking in feeling.
However, whilst withdrawal is likely to bring out feelings of sadness
and helplessness in others, intrusion is much more likely to evoke anger,
particularly when it appears that the person's way of relating or
conducting social interactions may be deliberately intended to upset or
hurt. These feelings are especially hard to keep in check if the person
has no outward signs of disability (this is true for most people identified
as autistic) and appears generally to be very able. In these circumstances
it can be difficult to remember that one of the most significant and

invisible areas of difficulty for the person is social relating, and that inappropriate ways of relating are unlikely to be deliberate, but are the result of deep seated difficulties in understanding and relating to the thoughts and feelings of others. It can sometimes take a lot of effort to get beyond that instinctive cry from the heart 'I don't care if he's got autism, he should know better!'

The links between social relating difficulties and behaviour

Human beings can only survive (physically and emotionally) as part of a social system. We have to effect 'social docking' if we are to learn, understand, solve problems, experience joy and pain, feel secure in ourselves, feel respected, have a valued role in society, laugh and have a well functioning immune system. There are many differences in the types of docking that works best – individual differences and cultural differences. These differences may be in the numbers of people engaged with, the types of interactions, the frequency of interactions, the importance assigned to specific relationships and interactions. Whilst there is no universally correct form of docking, long-term isolation (whether the result of withdrawal or rejection) is not a safe option for people.

Herein lies the cruellest of dilemmas for some people with autism. The social docking programmes built into others do not function so effectively for them. Their attempts to find a safe and secure social place often fail. For some, the problem may be compounded by the siren call of sensory pleasures. The social world is such a puzzle but the world of sensory experiences is such a joy, an easier focus in the short term. Thus lured by sensory excitements or driven by despair the person with autism may easily slip from social engagement and withdraw from the people around him.

Whatever short-term gain there may be from withdrawal becomes outweighed rapidly by the costs. It is hard to stay feeling well in isolation and withdrawal. More and more thoughts intrude, more and more things become obsessions and compulsions (see Chapter 8). The social world does not go away. Its intrusions become increasingly intolerable and lead to increasingly painful confrontations. As the individual slips more and more from social engagement the social world becomes more and more likely to identify that individual as challenging in terms of the behaviour that he shows. But a focus just upon the behaviour will miss the underlying process.

For others, of course, the problem is quite different. Their attempts at engaging socially, at forming relationships, may be intense but fraught with blunders and misunderstandings. At best, they may be perceived as irritating; at worst, cruel and spiteful. In these circumstances it is not the individual who withdraws from social contact but others who withdraw from the person because they find the behaviour hard to tolerate. As the individual tries ever harder to engage, the social world may become ever more likely to identify him as challenging.

Hence this chapter looks at how to build or rebuild positive social engagement. It is based upon the premise that if such social engagement can be effected, behaviour that others consider challenging will decrease. It is important to recognize that this is not a battle fought once and for all. It is a vital ingredient of the work to be done when the children are young. However the in-built difficulties (for all concerned) in sustaining successful social engagement mean that it is an issue that may need revisiting for some people with autism throughout their lives. They can slip easily from a hard won but fragile social place and rescue operations may need to be mounted if they are not to become lost in social isolation.

Effecting positive social engagement – building high-quality relationships

To feel and function well it is necessary to be embedded in a set of social relationships where a number of people think well of us, are there for us in times of trouble and who bring out good feelings in us. The quality of relationships is more important than the number and actual frequency of contacts. Relationships can be of many kinds – family, friends, acquaintances, mentors, those paid to provide regular services, those volunteering specific supports. A quality social system will be marked by a range of relationship types with more of the relationships being positive than neutral or negative.

There are certain characteristics common to all constructive social relationships. These include:

(1) *Unconditional positive regard.* Though I may object to some of the things that you do I retain a positive view of you as a person.

(2) *Positive social interactions and comments.* These occur more often than negative social encounters and comments.

(3) *Mutual trust and respect.* Not only do I respect, trust and value you but I work to ensure that you respect, trust and value me also.

(4) *Reciprocity.* Control and influence flow in both directions. Sometimes you determine what I do, sometimes I determine what you do. There is a balance. In conflict there is an attempt to find win–win outcomes, based upon compromise, rather than win–lose outcomes, which are based upon control.

(5) *Boundaries.* There are clear limits set so that each party can learn what is acceptable and unacceptable to the other.

There are two common challenges in building quality social support for people with autism, especially those who act in ways that cause concern for others. The first challenge is that there are likely to be too few people in the social system relating constructively with the individual. People may be rejecting her, constantly nagging or criticizing her about her behaviour and not focusing upon anything else. They may be responding to the behaviour by either becoming authoritarian or refusing to set limits. They may not be interacting at all with her – she may be left entirely to her own devices. The second challenge to building quality social supports is that the social system around the person may be too narrowly based. It may be worthwhile drawing a social map (Exercise 5.1).

Exercise 5.1

Drawing a Social Map

(1) Take a sheet of paper and place a symbol representing the person in the centre of the page.

(2) Around the person, place symbols representing all the people who are involved in the person's life, one symbol for family members, one for those paid to be there (staff), one symbol for 'others'.

This exercise often reveals graphically how dependent people with autism can be upon their family members and paid carers for their social interactions. Such dependence is likely to increase as the person moves from childhood to adulthood. It brings home the need to enrich the social support system around the person.

Enhancing social engagement, therefore, is about increasing the number of people involved and also increasing the frequency and success rate of a range of social interactions. There are a variety of ways in which social engagement can be improved. This may involve work in many areas. Not everyone will need work in all the areas. Indeed, some individuals whose behaviour is cause for concern may not need any work in the area of social relating. For those who do, however, priority areas of work will be determined by an assessment of individual need.

Building and sustaining empathy for the person

GENERAL PRINCIPLES

Empathy is about seeing and understanding someone else's world from his or her individual perspective, without necessarily sharing the same experience or framework oneself. It goes beyond sympathy. Empathy enables us to respect and value others regardless of whether we share their views or outlook. To practise empathy is to try to understand and remain non-judgemental about the frameworks a person uses to understand and interact with his social world. In general it means clearing one's mind of all other thoughts and feelings and focusing upon what is known about the other person and how it might feel to be operating in the world in that way. It requires imagination. It is hard. It may be particularly hard to gain and sustain empathy towards those people with autism whose behaviour we consider to be challenging or unacceptable. It remains important, nevertheless, to sustain the effort at empathy. Without empathy it will be hard to develop constructive relating which is a necessary part of the support to individuals.

TIPS AND HINTS

(1) All those paid to support the individual should receive autism-specific training, which should include facts, figures and theories. It should also include exposure to autobiographical writings of people with autism and the chance to meet people with autism who can speak about how life is from their point of view.

(2) When paid staff enter a person's life it is important that they get to know the person as a whole and have time to spend with the person doing things that he or she likes to do or at the least just time to observe and to listen.

(3) Those working and living with the person may need constant reminders about the social impairment which is involved in autism. This is especially true when a particular behaviour is hard to tolerate and when those involved start to personalize the issues ('He's doing it to upset me', 'He enjoys hurting people'). Such personalizing indicates a loss of insight into the difficulties that people identified as autistic have in recognizing and taking account of the thoughts and feelings of others.

Gregory, a young man in his early twenties, became aggressive and developed sexualized language and behaviour towards female staff. The impact of these behaviours upon staff's attitudes and morale was very powerful. They grew to dislike him and started avoiding spending time in his company. Their anger became so intense that they would not co-operate with strategies designed to help Gregory regain his previous positive focus. The staff started to believe that he was very aware of the emotional impact his behaviours were having upon them and that he took pleasure from upsetting and offending them and other service users living in the home. Intensive work needed to be done with the staff team (discussing, questioning, challenging, refresher training in autism) to help them regain a positive attitude, to reinstate their understanding of the nature of Gregory's social understanding difficulties and how this made it unlikely that he was deliberately upsetting them. Yes, he was aware that his behaviour had an impact – he realized that people told him off, asked him go to his room and did not talk to him. However, the likelihood that he really understood how his behaviour affected others' feelings was very low. Only by engaging in this kind of work with the staff team was it possible to move on in the work to provide positive support for Gregory.

(4) Those involved in the day-to-day life of someone who presents with serious behavioural challenges need access to people outside the system that they can talk to about their own difficulties and feelings. They need access to someone who can help them make sense of and plan practical strategies for managing behaviour and helping the person to move on.

Helping the person feel comfortable around social contact

GENERAL PRINCIPLES

Contact with others can be enormously stressful for some people identified as autistic. They often show tremendous courage in persevering with an experience that can be very overwhelming – people so close, making so much noise, touching, moving about. As long as there are compensations social contact can be sustained. But if there is no pleasure or comfort involved then withdrawal and avoidance are the logical solution.

Thus one aspect of work in this area is to help the individual to feel more comfortable around others, so that she can spend more time engaged in social contact. A second aspect of the work is to accept the difficulties that the person experiences with social contact and find ways to enable the person to withdraw safely and spend some time alone. This means structuring the use of time alone rather than allowing it to become a permanent state or to be a consequence that follows an unacceptable behaviour. The aim is not to turn the person into an extrovert party animal (this would be impossible, in any event) but to facilitate positive social engagement, at a level that works best for the particular individual who is being supported. It is to avoid the extremes of withdrawal and to make sure that problematic behaviour does not become or remain the means to achieving withdrawal.

TIPS AND HINTS

(1) If an individual is spending most of his or her time alone or at a distance from others, try to make brief contacts on a regular basis and build up from there. For example, schedule frequent brief 'visits' (a few minutes) and take small 'gifts' when visiting (small favoured items). If such brief social visits cause stress, reduce the pressure for any sort of active engagement during the visit. Impose on yourself a vow of silence to see if that helps the person tolerate your company better (it may help to bring a book to read or some paperwork to do). It may also be helpful to make minimal use of direct eye contact, relying instead on the use of peripheral vision.

(2) Use techniques described in the Options or Intensive Interaction methods. Spend regular time (up to 15 minutes, at least daily) with the person trying to join in what they are choosing to do (this may be a behaviour that some might label stereotypical or obsessional – for example, moving their hands in an eye-catching way, rocking, paper shredding). The idea is for you to engage with the person through imitating what the person does. If this stage is tolerated then you may at a later time try to introduce some variation to the activity and get the person to copy what you do. From here a more give and take, reciprocal interaction can develop with the two of you 'suggesting' things to each other.

(3) If the person has favoured activities that he will do with other people schedule these to occur more often.

(4) Schedule individual contact sessions but give the person a lot of concrete choices about what goes on – where the sessions occur, who sits or stand where (to give proximity control), whether an activity is done...or not, whether talking goes on...or not, whether we stop now...or not.

Sam moved out of his family home and into residential care at the age of 45 years. He was extremely anxious around people and would barricade himself in his room when other service users were in the house or when he was feeling especially tense. When the house was quiet, he might venture downstairs into the living room and listen to music, but would not want anyone else to come into the room. A strategy was adopted whereby staff would knock on the living room door approximately every hour and ask Sam if they might come in. Immediately they would ask Sam where he wished them to be – by the door or nearer to him, standing or sitting, speaking or remaining silent, looking at him or looking directly in front. Sam found this an amusing 'game' to play and it became possible in this way to gradually build up his tolerance of the presence of others. From there it became possible to develop more constructive forms of interaction.

(5) Structure into the person's daily schedule time away from others with access to preferred solitary activities.

(6) Try to provide 'safe havens' – places to which the individual can safely withdraw – for the times when he may become overwhelmed. Such 'safe havens' may need to be provided in all the main environments used by the person and the person informed that this is the place to which he can go.

Jason spent much of the school day in the toilet, escaping from the classroom whenever the opportunity arose. Attempts to bring him back to class often resulted in severe headbanging. It was felt that Jason was stressed by the hustle and bustle of the classroom and withdrew to the toilet to escape this. A walk-in cupboard in the classroom was converted into a quiet, safe area for Jason. His desk was placed directly in front of the cupboard (the door had been removed) so that he could withdraw into it whenever he felt the need. He soon stopped going off to the toilet area and used the safe area instead. Within a short while, he stopped withdrawing to this area also. As long as he knew it was there he felt safe and was able to engage with his education.

Earning trust and respect from the person

GENERAL PRINCIPLES

Trust and respect are a prerequisite for secure relating. They must be built, not assumed. The building of trust and respect involves a number of elements:

(1) The person needs to feel that we respect and value him. He needs to feel that we enjoy spending time with him. This can be difficult, particularly if his behaviour is very challenging. Some behavioural challenges can encourage avoidance of him, contacts become reduced to basic care (toileting, dressing, washing, feeding) and behaviour control ('Stop that', 'Don't do that'). They can become predominantly negative. The imbalance may need to be redressed if trust and respect are to be built.

(2) The person needs to know that we are consistent. People with autism often find other human beings confusing and puzzling and this may be one reason why they opt out of social contact. The problem, however, is partly of our making. People are inherently changeable and variable. One factor in human 'changeability' is our tolerance levels. These may fluctuate according to our physical and psychological state. As tolerance levels change, so does behaviour. When we feel on top form we may be able to tolerate high levels of noise, for example, but with a headache, we shout and tell people to be quiet. Such day-to-day inconsistency can be confusing to anyone, but it becomes a much greater issue for someone who has no means of understanding the causes. Another factor in the changeability of those who support a person is their judgement about the state of that person. If people judge the

individual to be 'in a good mood', they will expect more from him, make greater demands upon him. If they judge the person to be 'in a bad mood', fewer demands will be made. This is perfectly reasonable at one level but from the perspective of the person identified as autistic it adds to the unpredictability of the world. Thus extra effort is required to offer support in a consistent way. It is a vital accommodation to the 'disability' that we call autism. It also helps to build secure relationships.

(3) The person needs to know that we can control our emotional responses and remain focused. People with autism labels can often experience heightened arousal and emotional distress and this is a factor in many behavioural incidents. In such a state, when loss of control is a possibility, the individual needs people around him who can remain calm, clear, firm and in control of their own emotional responses. This is critical for helping the individual regain a more comfortable, calm state and avoid the terrible experience of loss of control. People with autism are very sensitive to changes in other people's behaviour. They pick up the feelings of those around them. If our own anxieties escalate and we begin to panic, their distress will be compounded and this, in turn, will undermine the quality of their relationship with us.

(4) The person needs to be able to understand what we are communicating. We have discussed earlier the problems that individuals with autism can have in making sense of certain communication styles – language full of abstracts, idioms, short cuts – where some of the message is expressed and the rest has to be inferred. The problems can be magnified when meaning has also to be derived from additional cues such as gestures, facial expressions or tone of voice (for example, the simple phrase 'What are you doing' will take on a completely differently meaning, according to which word in the phrase is accentuated). Further confusions can occur when others joke or tease. In so far as we can accommodate to the person's difficulties and develop concrete and explicit ways of

communicating it will strengthen our overall relationship with the person (and, also, make us generally more effective communicators).

TIPS AND HINTS

(1) Keep a count of the types of interactions that the person receives. Ensure that social contacts with the person are predominantly positive ones. For any one negative interaction there should be at least four or five positive interactions, as a minimum. If the ratio is less than this it is an indication that action is needed if constructive relationships are to be built and sustained.

(2) Spend time regularly with the person engaging in her preferred activities – so that the relationship is not just focused on teaching, basic care tasks or behaviour management (*our* support agenda). Go for a walk together, do a jigsaw puzzle together, listen to music together, spin things together!

(3) Some people are not able to engage in an activity whilst under pressure to engage socially. Thus, if the person finds it difficult or stressful to engage socially, then minimize the social input during activities so that concentration is not undermined and success and enjoyment are more likely.

Jake, a young adult living in a residential care home, loved to go out for walks. He would take himself out several times a day for a long walk. However, he had phases during which he experienced high levels of anxiety. During one of these phases it was discovered that he had been kicking down fences and stealing from shops whilst out on his walks. The obvious response was to have staff accompany him on walks. Jake soon lost interest in these accompanied walks and his anxiety state increased. It emerged that staff accompanying him on the walks would always try to engage him in conversation. Once it was decided to walk in silence with him, Jake regained his interest and pleasure in going for walks.

(4) When spending time with an individual offer choices about whether to talk or remain silent. If sitting with someone offer choices about where the person sits and where you sit.

(5) Show a high level of personal consistency – in your moods, in the boundaries that you set, in the expectations that you have of the person. Try making a 'consistency list' – a list of the things that you will always try to do and a list of the things you will try always not to do.

(6) Linked to the previous point, develop a 'communication list', the things that you will always try to do/not to do when engaging in any form of communication with the individual.

(7) For some people, you may need to reduce direct eye contact or physical touching during your time with them.

(8) Pay particular attention to how you use language with the individual. Verbally presented information needs to be clear, literal and unambiguous (see Chapter 4).

(9) Humour and laughter are an important part of relating but be careful in the use of social humour. The person may interpret jokes literally and become distressed or angry. Use slapstick rather than irony.

(10) Be persistent. If the person rejects social contact, we must persist on a regular and consistent basis in our attempts to engage the person.

Encouraging the person to initiate social contact more often

GENERAL PRINCIPLES

A person may only rarely initiate social contact because he has not realized that other people can be helpful. Initiation may be rare because contact is aversive and likewise the person may respond to initiations from others with behaviour that is of concern because contact with others may be associated with uncomfortable feelings. In such situations raising the frequency of initiations is a very important outcome to work towards. This means, for example, finding more ways in which other people can be useful or pleasurable to the person. The aim is for the initiation of social contact to achieve positive outcomes for the individual. There is an overlap with work to build trust and respect and, as with all the ideas presented in this book, the specific interventions put into practice will depend upon the individual – the goal is the same but the means will vary.

TIPS AND HINTS

(1)   Offer as many things as possible throughout the day (food, clothes, activities) in the form of concrete choices (that is, with the objects or understood symbols for them physically present).

(2)   If using a choices approach, sometimes offer the non-chosen option so that the person gets the chance to point out how inattentive you are by rejecting the item you are offering and indicating again the preferred item. This needs to be done carefully so that the individual is not angered.

(3)   Set up pleasurable activities which can be easily interrupted – for example, with young children swinging games, with older people playing music for them. The idea is to get the activity going and then introduce pauses with the idea of stimulating the person to initiate for you to continue.

(4)   Spend time quietly observing the person and when she is seen to be in difficulty sorting out a problem, step in to assist. With small children it is possible to put highly favoured items in sight but out of reach and as they look towards the item, make this a cue for interaction, when you will help them sort out the problem.

(5)   Wear clothes, jewellery or perfumes that you know will attract the individual so that the person approaches to look, smell and maybe touch (all within acceptable bounds of course!)

(6)   If the person likes small items that are easy to carry around with you (particular types of paper or material, perfumes or creams, small food items), always carry these and initially offer them to the person without any initiation so that they realize that you are the source of these favoured objects. Then

give them out less often to see if that will trigger more initiation to you.

(7) Use techniques described in the Options or Intensive Interaction methods, as described in an earlier section. This is a very useful approach for all sorts of social interaction difficulties but may certainly help to increase initiation rates.

Encouraging the person to co-operate more readily with reasonable requests

GENERAL PRINCIPLES

Behavioural difficulties may be accompanied by a more general diffi-culty with enlisting co-operation. Attempts to enlist co-operation may directly trigger behavioural incidents or very large amounts of effort may be required to enlist minimal amounts of co-operation. This effectively reduces social engagement. Sometimes this is not immed-iately obvious. If there are difficulties gaining co-operation our behaviour may be shaped to only make available those things that the person would do anyway. This creates an illusion of co-operation – the person remains busy and active but in fact the role of social input is negligible. The individual would engage in these activities whether or not anyone else was around or involved.

> *Anna loved to draw. She particularly enjoyed drawing buildings –*
> *most often, she would draw her school or house. Attempts to engage her*
> *in any other educational activities resulted in biting and headbanging.*
> *To avoid confrontations, or when there were problems with other*
> *students, Anna would be left to draw – sometimes with staff sitting by*
> *her. Anna's interactions with staff at these times consisted only of*
> *repetitive questions about the pictures she was drawing. It became clear*
> *that Anna was spending more and more time drawing and questioning*
> *without any positive developments occurring – no new things were*
> *drawn, no new topics of conversation developed. Anna gave the*
> *illusion of co-operation, but only because this was an activity which*
> *she would engage in endlessly anyway if given the opportunity.*

A total lack of social co-operation is not a safe or viable life option and a key target in such situations will be to raise the frequency of co-operation. This does of course raise ethical issues. The requests for co-operation need to be reasonable, in the sense that they further the interests of the individual or protect the rightful interests of others. Others will have legitimate claims on the co-operation of the person with autism – examples might include the TV channel watched in family or shared living situations, noise made at night which interferes with the sleep of others, interfering with the learning of others in school. Such decisions are particularly difficult when supporting adults with whom it is hard to discuss the issues. It is therefore important to use all the normal ethical safeguards when deciding what are reasonable requests to make of people. However, some there must be and once these are identified there are a number of possibilities for raising the success rate of these transactions.

TIPS AND HINTS

(1) Start with a small number of limited requests that are made consistently and put effort into seeing these through.

(2) Integrate requests into overall schedule planning or timetabling (see Chapter 4) so that the person is better able to predict what to expect, when to expect it and what follows after.

(3) Plan favoured activities to follow less favoured requested activities.

(4) Use the approaches to scheduling and timetabling discussed in Chapter 4 so that people get to know when things that are important to them will happen. If you want them to stop particular activities now, they must know that they can return to these later in the day.

(5) Embed a non-favoured requested activity within three or four favoured requested activities where the likelihood of co-operation is high. For example: take a drink (favoured activity), come and sit next to me (favoured activity), read the

words underneath the picture (non-favoured activity), colour in this picture (favoured activity).

(6) Change the medium in which requests are made – for example write them down, put them into the visual schedule system.

(7) Present requested activities in a choice format where you determine the choices but the person remains able to exert some control. For example 'Do you want to wash in the upstairs or downstairs bathroom' rather than 'It's time to wash'; 'Shall we clear out the newspapers you have hoarded above our agreed limit after breakfast or before dinner?' rather than 'You must clear out some of your newspapers'.

(8) Use a timer device to indicate the end of an activity. Sometimes lack of co-operation reflects not being sure when an activity might end. Having a concrete end signal may help the person co-operate with an activity, particularly if time on task starts very short and then builds up gradually.

(9) Directly reward the person for successful co-operation.

Setting limits

GENERAL PRINCIPLES

We have already emphasized that constructive relationships involve clear boundaries and that raises a number of important issues.

(1) It may be necessary to start setting limits because none are being set. This sometimes occurs in environments where a fuzzy and bizarre notion of 'choice' results in the users of a service having few or no boundaries set for them.

(2) Caregivers may vary in what limits are set and how they are set. Limit setting may be determined by individual's tolerance levels on the day and personal standards, which may vary from one person to the next. Whilst this is normal, such inconsistency stresses severely the coping capacities of people with autism.

(3) For some people the setting of limits triggers incidents of behaviour. As a result, fewer and fewer limits are set over time. The issue here is *how* to set limits for the person.

Supporting people in relation to behavioural issues can raise for us the need to identify what limits need to be set, how these limits are to be communicated and how we can effect a high degree of consistency in the setting of agreed limits.

TIPS AND HINTS

(1) If the person is at a stage where no limits are being set, decide on one area where limits will be set. Focus on this area only. It may be that constructive social engagement requires more limits to be observed but, using the principle of graded change, it is better to work consistently on one area and then move on to others rather than engaging in too many confrontations all at one go.

(2) Use the approaches to scheduling described in Chapter 4 so that the person can come to know when things important to her will happen – this will make it easier for her to accept a limit on the current activity.

(3) Develop a set of 'house rules' for acceptable and unacceptable behaviours, which are easily available and in visual format. These rules, which are for everyone, should be brief lists of between three and five key behaviours which are acceptable and the same for those that are unacceptable. Reminders of the rules should be given routinely as well as at the point when the rule is about to be or has just been broken. These rules are for everyone.

(4) When setting limits use an assertive style. Do not be aggressive (do not shout, do not grab hold of people, do not crowd them) but do not shrink from what you are doing. Gain the person's attention, speak clearly, use concrete language and positive directions (avoiding the words 'no' and 'don't') to tell the person what you want to happen now. Give the person time to respond but if necessary repeat (in words,

signs or pictures) what you want to happen now. If the limit is about the person wanting something that is in itself reasonable but cannot be provided now, indicate when the wanted event can occur (in words or by reference to the visual schedule) but always try to back this up by what the person needs to do now.

(5) If the person becomes increasingly aroused emotionally during limit setting try to refocus him on to what you want him to do now (distraction). If he becomes over-aroused withdraw yourself to give extra space and quiet or encourage him to withdraw to a quieter or more spacious area. If he has learned a specific technique for calming (going for a walk, going on a swing, tearing paper) encourage him to use that now (again, a positive direction).

Establishing relationship boundaries

GENERAL PRINCIPLES

Behavioural difficulties can occur because the person wants very much to relate to others but does not understand relationship boundaries – rules for physical contact, the difference between care, friendship and intimacy. Lack of boundaries may be the problem (some people tolerate unacceptable types of contact) or attempts to set boundaries may trigger more problematic behaviour. Thus for some individuals steps may need to be taken to make relationship boundaries very clear.

TIPS AND HINTS

(1) Provide clear rules and explanations about physical contact. For example, we shake hands to say hello – we do not cuddle; if you know a person, and they agree, it is OK to kiss them on the cheek the first time you see them in the day; when talking to people, stand at arm's length, keep your hands by your sides.

(2) Avoid sharing information about your own personal relationships as a way of trying to teach the person about relationships. Use general examples.

(3) Avoid private informal conversations about personal issues if there is any risk that this might be misunderstood. Formalize such contacts by allocating specific times and a specific person; structure the session.

Extending the network of social supports

GENERAL PRINCIPLES

Many people with autism are socially isolated in the sense of having a limited number of people in their lives fulfilling a limited number of roles. Some clearly describe their feelings of loneliness. Social isolation is a particular problem for those who present with serious behavioural challenges. It is important, therefore, to try to extend the number and diversity of social supports. This can be effected through two key strategies.

The first strategy is to draw more people into the 'circle of support' for the individual. This will not occur by chance, nor will it occur just through the person 'being' in the company of others. It needs to be planned for and encouraged in a structured way. The second strategy is to teach the person more effective social skills so that it becomes easier for him to draw people into his network. The topic of skill teaching is covered more extensively in Chapter 7. We mention it here to emphasize the importance of social skills in the development and maintenance of social relationships.

One way to develop social skills is to identify the individual's interests, ambitions and preferences, decide which of those involve doing something with other people and work out what skills the person needs in order to access those opportunities successfully. Access skills may be of two kinds. There are task skills (such as work, game or administrative skills) and social skills (conversational, listening, questioning, sharing). In preparing a person to access an opportunity, attention must be given to skill building in both areas. If the goal is to learn basketball, then the focus is not just on learning the ball skills and game rules, but on how to listen to the coach, what to talk about in the locker room, how to help a team mate who is angry. Another way to develop a person's social skills is to examine those social opportunities already available to the person but where things tend to go wrong; then to analyze the skills and competencies that the person needs in order to make those opportunities work more successfully from a social point of view. Strategies can be devised involving either new situations that the person is going to access or current situations where the focus is on improving the quality of access. The skills to teach will be those which raise the likelihood that the person will engage successfully at a social level.

TIPS AND HINTS

(1) Use the person's skills and interests and the paid support available to help her to access social situations where others may be drawn into her life – examples would include employment, volunteering, joining a 'hobby' club, getting a fitness trainer or sports coach. Care and active support is needed in all these situations to make such engagements successful. However, these are often very fruitful avenues for bringing new people into the person's circle of support.

(2) In group situations such as school, the workplace or clubs it may help to formalize a 'buddy group', people who are willing to join the individual and work to develop their relationships. Such a group needs to be planned, facilitated and to meet regularly to review how things are going, to problem solve around difficult issues. Such systems increase the likelihood of constructive support developing, compared to a 'place and hope' approach.

(3) Explore the possibilities for 'paid volunteering' (John Shea, personal communication) as an alternative to staff support for some activities, particularly as the person reaches adulthood. For example, if the person loves to run or attend Star Trek conventions and needs only a minimal level of support to access these situations, then offering generous expenses may help to draw in someone from outside and this may enable a relationship to develop. Again, caution is needed in recruiting and supporting people but this can be an avenue for broadening social support as well as enriching general quality of life.

(4) Teach only those skills that the person is going to use *now.*
Teach to specific, current situations and teach specific skills to
manage these specific situations. Do not try to teach generic,
flexible skills – those may emerge over time but you cannot
be too specific in the skills that you teach and the situations
you teach for.

(5) Never assume that a skill taught in one situation will
generalize to another situation. Always give specific practice
in any situation where the skill is appropriate.

(6) Make sure that teaching emphasizes actual practice. Role-play
may be useful in building up skills but always support the
person into using the skill in the actual real life situation.

(7) Teach specific 'rules' for what to do in specific social
situations. These may be used inflexibly and sometimes rather
oddly but it is better for the person to master specific rules for
situations because trying to teach flexible problem solving
and reading of social situations tends to be much less
successful.

(8) Provide portable reminders or prompts for the rules taught
(for example cue cards, audio tapes) so that the person has a
resource to fall back on if anxiety or misunderstanding
interferes with his functioning in the situation. This will give
him much more independence than training the skills and
hoping that he will recall them at the moment when they are
needed.

Concluding remarks

Maintaining constructive social engagement is a long-term issue for
people with autism and an important theme in enabling people to
function in a way that does not get them identified as challenging.
Difficulties may arise because the person does not know how to engage
socially, because the person has lost focus and drifted off to other
priorities or because the person has lost that sense of well being and
withdrawn from the world. Whatever the additional needs that may be
implicated in a lack of social engagement it is our view that although

such engagement is very challenging for people with autism the alternative is much worse – without engagement it proves impossible to sustain learning, development, tolerance and well being. More and more internal intrusions occur, more and more compulsions overwhelm the individual. This leads to more and more behaviours that others will identify as challenging and this in its turn will generate more and more difficulties – more social rejection, more likelihood of unpredicted changes (moves of house, changes in support staff), more likelihood of powerful drugs with unpleasant side effects. The battle to maintain and to enhance social engagement is the battle to cut into this downward spiral. It is a battle to be fought at many levels. The battle may need to be fought and re-fought many times throughout the person's lifetime.

CHAPTER 6

Well Being

What this chapter is about

A number of people with autism appear to have difficulties sustaining a sense of personal well being. Their behaviour worsens in frequency and intensity when their well being is reduced. We use a clumsy phrase like well being because the needs of the person are often expressed in a mixture of physical and emotional ways – the person who lacks well being may be physically unwell, emotionally upset or both (we do not wish to prejudge whether one is more important than the other, whether one causes the other or whether both reflect an underlying more holistic concept). This chapter looks at the relationship between personal well being and behaviour and the things that can be done to improve personal well being when this is thought to be a contributory factor to problematic behaviour.

Identifying well being issues

The detection of reduced well being can be difficult. The external signs may not be obvious and reporting on subjective states can be difficult. People with no language skills will obviously find such reporting difficult; but even those with good language skills can find it hard to understand and/or describe their internal states, whether emotional or physical. This is an area of huge difficulty for many who carry the label of autism. There may be additional barriers – some may refuse medical or dental examinations. So behaviour may be the most immediately detectable sign that something is wrong.

What actually is wrong will vary. Reduced well being may involve one or more of the following:

○ A clearly diagnosable physical problem, either discrete (for example, tooth or gum infection) or recurring (for example, constipation, hay fever, throat or ear infection).

○ A sense from those who know the person well that there is a physical problem even though the nature of the problem cannot be pinned down (the idea of 'one degree under').

○ A way of emotional being in the world that is marked by a negative bias. This can be seen through the emotions that the person expresses (anger, distress, anxiety or gloom); the subjects that the person talks intensely about (how bad he is, what a failure he is, how no one likes him); the memories upon which the person dwells (the bad things he has done or that have happened to him); the infrequency with which the person smiles or is seen to be happy and relaxed. This is a general approach to the world – a matter of temperament and style, rather than a temporary difficulty.

○ A way of emotional being in the world which is marked by constant anxiety. This can be seen through physical signs (poor concentration, inability to settle, sweating, pacing, muscular tension) and behavioural signs (continual seeking of reassurance about what is happening, who is around, when particular events will occur, specific worries). This, again, may be a general way of being in the world rather than a temporary difficulty.

○ An extended phase of reduced well being, marked by a loss of a previous state in which more positive feelings and behaviours were evident. Sometimes this may be a discrete phase following significant events, such as losses, bereavements, moves. Sometimes it may be a recurring pattern. Some people show clear and marked cycles in their behaviour and well being. They have positive phases and negative phases. These phases are extended in time (more than just normal moodiness) and the down phases are very marked. These phases may recur on a cyclical or seasonal basis or may occur in response to changes and upheavals in the person's life. Such phases may be marked by physical illness, lowered mood, sleep disturbance, appetite change, increased anxiety, reduced tolerance, increased compulsiveness and increases in aggression or self injury.

○ An extended phase of reduced well being, onsetting in adolescence or early adulthood (as opposed to the alternating cycles described above). This is a marked break from how the person functioned early in life. This will manifest in obvious emotional distress, a withdrawal from activities and an unwillingness to accept any limits being set, sometimes a loss of skills. Anger is often a prominent feature. Our clinical experience is that the phase can last a number of years in contrast to the cycles that may last weeks or months. It does pass, however, if appropriate support is provided.

○ A clear and diagnosable depression which does not fit the above characterizations.

The area of well being is a prominent area of need for many of those whose behaviour presents serious challenges to service provision.

How lack of well being may contribute to behaviour that is challenging

We think of well being, or more specifically lack of well being, as operating in a number of ways which are probably related.

(1) Lack of well being may alter the motivational biases of the individual. It reduces tolerance to everyday pressures – pressures from the physical environment (noise, heat, crowding), from the social environment, pressures from activities which must be engaged in. It causes more things to be experienced as painful, irritating or intrusive. The motivation to escape from everyday pressures or to drive the intrusions away, to terminate the unpleasantness or pain is increased. Behaviours that achieve these results accelerate.

(2) Lack of well being may alter how the person thinks about the world. Other people may be seen as deliberately trying to harm the person or put her down or exert undue control and therefore need to be stopped (for example, by attacking them) or escaped from (for example, by running away). Alternatively

the person may come to think of herself as worthless, defective, responsible for her own problems and imperfections and this may lead to self-destructive behaviours.

(3) Lack of well being may be accompanied by heightened emotionality. Heightened arousal levels reduce the threshold for catastrophic emotional outbursts. The person becomes distressed more easily and more intensely. Rapid increases in arousal lead to rapid loss of control. The expression of this may be behaviours such as aggression, self injury or destructiveness.

(4) Lack of well being impairs other key inhibitory resources. Thus in Tourette's disorder and obsessive compulsive disorder the frequency, duration and intensity of 'uncontrolled' movements and 'uncontrollable' behaviours will increase when the person is stressed. Some of these movements and behaviours may well be regarded as challenging (the more 'driven' or 'compulsive' forms of aggression and self injury, for example). This is as yet an area where the actual mechanisms and relationships are poorly understood but clinical experience suggests that the concept of inhibition/ disinhibition may be a useful perspective upon some of the behavioural challenges that we face. When others try to stop the movements or limit the rituals, behavioural outbursts may follow.

(5) The coping mechanisms that the individual adopts when experiencing lack of well being create secondary problems. For example, the person may withdraw from all activities and shut himself away in his bedroom. He may stop speaking to those around him. Such behaviours can become habitual, part of the routine of being in the world and result in loss of social engagement (see Chapter 5). Trying to address these behaviours directly without addressing well being is unlikely to lead to successful outcomes.

Whichever mechanisms are involved in linking lack of well being to behaviour, the basic theme is clear. The more that we can improve and sustain an individual's well being the less likely he or she will be to show the behaviours of concern. This has implications for how we help people who have lost their sense of well being. It has very important implications, as yet unexplored, for prevention.

Strategies for promoting well being

There are a number of general strategies which will address needs in the area of well being. These fall into the broad domain usually identified by the term 'quality of life'. In so far as the person can be supported into a good quality of life this will assist in restoring those who have lost a sense of well being and will help to sustain well being in those who may be vulnerable to its loss. The areas that contribute to the experience of quality of life include physical and mental health, positive emotional state (positive mood, high self esteem and contentment), a network of high quality social supports and a lifestyle which is meaningful and which delivers success and enjoyment. We will consider each of these areas in turn.

(A) Quality of physical health

GENERAL PRINCIPLES

It will be important to ensure good physical health. This involves vigilance on the part of carers to pick up changes in the behaviour of the individual, changes that may be the first indication that something is wrong. Maintaining good physical health involves ready access to the full range of medical services, so that ordinary health problems can be picked up and treated as quickly as possible. It involves access to well man/well woman services, lifestyle adjustments in terms of diet, supplements and exercise or such activities as yoga and meditation. Access to good dental care is vital. People with autism often have very restricted, self-imposed diets, and may also resist or lack the skills of everyday dental care. This may lead to increased rates of tooth and gum problems.

Quality of health also means keeping a close watch on the developing research that may lead to a better understanding of the specific

physical vulnerabilities of some people with autism. Promising ideas at
the time of writing relate to difficulties in the functioning of the
immune system and whether this can be boosted by immunoglobulin
injections; and difficulties in metabolic functioning particularly in
relation to gluten and/or casein. Some people may be sensitive to
particular colourings or additives in food. There is also a question
about whether some have undiagnosed bowel or gut disease. Indeed,
bowel functioning, especially the problem of constipation, recurs as a
particular health challenge for a significant number of people with
autism. At the very least this urges attention to diet, whatever else is
done. Other common health challenges include seasonal allergies and
recurring ear infections which may have no obvious external signs
(sinus or ear pain) and which require close attention, especially if the
individual's health history indicates vulnerability in these areas.

Finally, we include here the question of mental health. People with
autism, like all people, need to be able to access competent help in this
area if they are experiencing a mental health problem that is treatable by
recognized means. They need the same kinds of mental health support
as others. There is no evidence for them having 'special' mental health
problems and there is certainly no evidence to justify the frequent use of
powerful medication just for their behaviour. The justification for
medication is the same as it is for other people – the person is
experiencing a condition that research indicates is demonstrably improved by competent use of specific medications. The most common
conditions are depression, anxiety, obsessive-compulsive disorder and
Tourette's syndrome (which is more a neurological problem than
strictly 'mental health'). 'Attention deficit' terms may also be applied to
people with autism. Less common are extreme mood swings from high
to low (manic-depression, bi-polar affective disorder) and schizo-
phrenia.

TIPS AND HINTS

(1) Check routinely for the presence of minor ailments – colds
    and catarrh, seasonal allergies, problems with feet,
    constipation or wind, sleep disturbance, discomfort from
    effects of heat, headaches.

(2) Arrange regular physical and dental check ups.

(3) In consultation with the person's mainstream medical practitioners, consider the use of complementary medicine for those who have recurring vulnerability to specific ailments.

(4) If a person is unwell, consider whether routines should be maintained despite the fact that the person may not be fully up to the routines.

Frank had been showing a steady increase in aggressive behaviour over some months, with a more dramatic increase over a three-week period. It was discovered that Frank was suffering with haemorrhoids. Urgent treatment was sought. Meanwhile, and despite his physical discomfort, it was felt important to maintain Frank's everyday routines in order to avoid any additional increase in anxiety (Frank found any changes in routine intensely anxiety provoking).

(5) For those who drink a lot – tea, coffee, coke – the removal of caffeine from the diet may be important. Caffeine induces physiological changes similar to those that accompany anxiety and agitation, especially when taken in large quantities.

(6) Consider food supplements for those whose diets are poor because of self-restrictions.

(7) Regular physical exercise contributes to overall well being (physical and emotional). Because this contribution can be so significant, the subject is given fuller consideration in the next section.

(B) Quality of emotional well being/personal satisfaction

Emotional well being includes positive mood state, comfortable energy level, a balance favouring positive over negative emotions, a sense of the self as valuable and satisfaction with most areas of life. Its promotion involves attention to factors within the individual and life outside. In this section we will consider more direct influences on individual state. In the next two sections we will consider external promoters of well being – the quality of the social support system and the quality of the activities that go to make up the person's lifestyle.

Physical exercise

GENERAL PRINCIPLES

A very significant contributor to the promotion of both physical and emotional well being is exercise. This is an area in which a large amount of general research as well as more specific research in relation to behaviour has been undertaken. Both research and experience indicate that regular, structured aerobic exercise that builds fitness makes a positive contribution to emotional and physical well being. For this to occur it is necessary to identify a form of exercise that the person at least tolerates and, even better, enjoys! Fortunately many (but not all) people with autism enjoy physical activities – swimming, cycling, hiking, skating, climbing, aerobics. The key is to find an activity which can become part of the person's lifestyle, which means that it is engaged in frequently (several times a week). This will mean assigning a higher priority to exercise than is usual in some programmes or curricula. Support may be needed from the person's doctor and the advice of a fitness coach will be helpful in planning the individual's programme. There are immediate short-term benefits from physical exercise. In the time immediately following exercise (between half an hour and three hours) the person may be happier, more relaxed, less focused on self-stimulatory activities, more able to concentrate. There are long-term benefits too – enhanced mood, a decrease in irritability/arousability and better health.

TIPS AND HINTS

(1) It may be necessary to look carefully at the attitudes of those who support the person, particularly if the person needs a lot of support. Access to physical exercise can be easily blocked if those who support the person themselves dislike exercise in general or exercise in the particular form favoured by the individual.

(2) Some exercise programmes involve intense phases of activity. This can be a little overwhelming for some. It is important, therefore, to follow intense phases with a cool down/unwind phase so that arousal levels can be brought down before engaging the individual in new activities. This will avoid increasing the risk of problematic behaviours associated with heightened arousal.

(3) Ensure that the exercise activity is structured. Unstructured exercise (such as pacing, running around) can lead to increases in excitability, with no benefit to emotional well being and behavioural functioning.

(4) Use special interests to increase the motivation to exercise. For example, use favoured music, an interest in numbers or routes; link exercise machines to the delivery of preferred visual stimulation.

Relaxation

GENERAL PRINCIPLES

Although there is research on the general benefits of regular relaxation (for example, through yoga, meditation or progressive muscular relaxation) there is less specific research in relation to how this may impact on the emotions and behaviour of people with autism. Clinical experience suggests that many people with autism labels have difficulty achieving a relaxed state but if they are assisted to do so, this can have positive outcomes on mood, anxiety level and behaviour. However, we would stress the need for more research in this area.

There are a number of ways of helping someone to access a relaxed state. The first is through direct relaxation induction. This usually requires attention to body positioning (sitting or lying rather than standing or moving about); a reduction in external stimulation (minimum noise and lowered lighting levels); a dominant repetitive stimulus (for example, music or chanting). In addition to these general considerations there may be specific additional strategies – for example, breathing, massage of body areas, holding of acupressure points, use of specific aromas (aromatherapy), use of specific music held to have intrinsic relaxing qualities.

Some people are so physically tense that relaxation induction may not achieve the desired effects during the initial sessions. People may need time to get used to what is happening and to respond. There will also be many individual differences in the circumstances which effect a relaxed state and it is important to accommodate to these – some people may react adversely to the strategies which are commonly used in direct relaxation induction. Thus a person may become very anxious in a darkened room or if asked to close her eyes, or she may become very excited by music or aroma.

Achieving a relaxed state may have a stand-alone benefit – the person enjoys the experience and this adds to the number of positive experiences in a day. However, carry over effects from the session may be very limited, the person's anxiety or tension returning soon after the session. Thus for people with chronic and pervasive anxiety it may be necessary to schedule several sessions a day if a meaningful impact upon functioning is to be made.

The alternative to direct relaxation induction is to teach the person over a series of sessions some specific skills which can help him to relax and be less tense. The three best known approaches to this are yoga, meditation and progressive muscular relaxation. Progressive muscular relaxation involves working systematically through all the major muscle groups in the body, encouraging the person to relax each muscle in turn. The relaxation process is linked to a focus on breathing so that steady, controlled breathing is incorporated into the relaxation routine. The outcome of this and other approaches to relaxation induction is that over time the individual learns how to relax himself. By learning to monitor and reduce tension the person is then able to use this skill in situations where arousal or anxiety start to overwhelm.

TIPS AND HINTS

(1) Although many people with autism are sensitive to touch, they often respond well to massage and acupressure.

(2) Find a way to measure objectively the person's level of tension. By measuring tension prior to the relaxation session and then immediately after the session the impact of the session can be judged. The duration of any positive impact

should also be measured. This will help to judge how often, if at all, sessions should be scheduled in a day.

(3) Tension can be measured by observation of muscle tension, sweat levels on palms or forehead, breathing or pulse rate. Some people may be able to rate the level of their own tension, using a rating scale. It may be helpful to try to find an interesting visual representation of how much tension is felt (for example, balloons of different sizes).

(4) Teaching steady and controlled breathing can be especially difficult. Try using balloons, bubbles, windmills or musical instruments to help the person learn how to take steady breaths and slowly breathe out.

(5) During regular relaxation induction sessions, introduce a distinctive and highly portable cue to signal the start of the session (for example, a particular word, a special picture, a distinctive aroma). Over time the cue itself may come to be associated with a relaxed state. It can then be made available in the person's everyday environments and used to help 'on the spot' calming when the person starts to become tense.

Inducting positive mood

Mood is one of the most commonly used explanations for behavioural difficulties. Yet it is often treated as though it has a life of its own and is not subject to influence. Everyday experience and a body of literature in general psychology indicates that mood can be positively influenced in rather straightforward ways, although the effects of such mood enhancement can be relatively short lived. It may therefore be helpful to schedule inputs to promote positive mood to occur several times a day. It is no good waiting until the person is in a bad mood and then trying to cheer him up. It is far better to be proactive and schedule regular inputs to enhance mood. Such inputs can be direct or indirect.

Direct mood induction means doing something with the person that has an immediate and very direct effect upon mood. It is important to be clear about what mood one is aiming for. Two broad positive mood areas are being pleasurably relaxed and being amused. Inducting

a pleasurably relaxed mood state may be effected through the relaxation activities described above. Other ways to achieve this mood state
are brief periods (approximately 10 minutes) of vigorous exercise (such
as a brisk walk) or time alone on a repetitive activity. An amused mood
may be inducted by jokes, horseplay, videos or even by just practising
the physical act of smiling.

The effects of such strategies on positive mood are only likely to last
for a relatively short period, maybe 10–60 minutes. But that may be
enough, particularly if the strategies are used several times in a day, to
get the person through and enable him to cope better whilst longer-
term work is undertaken to address more major needs. When working
directly on positive mood induction it is important to identify the mood
that you want to bring out, identify the means to do that and any
resources required (for example the most effective forms of massage
require access to someone properly trained in these skills), then
schedule frequent sessions. This kind of work can easily be woven
informally into everyday life.

Indirect mood induction means doing things that do not necessarily
trigger an instant change but over time contribute to the person
experiencing a more positive mood. These also require careful planning
and scheduling although, once again, it is easy to weave this work into
everyday life. Indirect approaches to positive mood induction include
positive monitoring, positive reminiscence and increasing success experiences. Positive monitoring works to focus the attention of the person
on her positive feelings as a way of counteracting the tendency to dwell
on negative feelings. This may be effected by giving feed back on the
person's positive feelings – for example, by commenting on them
whenever a positive mood is apparent, using Polaroid snaps, a mirror or
video. It may be effected by helping the person herself to keep track of
her positive feelings (filling out positive mood rating forms, keeping a
diary of positive events, moods and experiences).

Positive reminiscence is likewise targeted to counteract the tendency of some people to dwell upon the negative experiences from their
past. It involves spending regular time with the person going over the
positive past – for example looking at videos of enjoyed occasions,
going through photograph albums or collected items, reviewing personal journals, reminding the person directly about good things that

have happened and the successes. Again, these kinds of supports are only likely to have an impact if planned to occur on a regular basis rather than in response to a bad mood or a person ruminating on the bad things that have happened.

Increasing success experiences relates to the fact that in a low mood state an individual's belief system can change. The person can come to believe that he is worthless and incompetent, that good things that happen are nothing to do with his own efforts. The work focuses upon increasing the opportunities for success in the person's everyday life in ways that can be attributed to his own contribution. This may mean reducing the complexity of demands, simply commenting more often on successes, showing appreciation more often for contributions made by him or providing some other feedback to him (for example, ticking off on a checklist tasks completed, feeding back work productivity figures).

TIPS AND HINTS

(1) Develop an objective means of judging mood state – a list of signs that all can recognize.

(2) Develop a list of the specific things that trigger positive mood in the individual and that amuse him and set targets for the number of times in a day that you want to see the person smile.

(3) Remember the idea of the transition ritual – brief exercises or some other input (for example a specific piece of music) – that is always used after one activity finishes and before the next one begins. This may diffuse arousal build up and help establish a positive approach to the next situation.

(4) Talking about feelings does not relieve those feelings. Talking is good for solving problems but if you want to shift a mood state quickly, don't talk…do.

(5) Non-contingent reinforcement (see Chapter 10) can be helpful for enhancing low mood. This increases the number of pleasurable activities the person engages in each day.

(6)   Schedule 'special activities', things for the person to look forward to. Care is needed here because too much warning is stressful for many people with autism. Develop the idea of a 'surprise' or 'mystery trip' or 'special award', the details of which will only be revealed at the last moment.

Christopher lost interest in all activities following the birth of his baby sister. He became aggressive at school and at home. In consultation with the family it was decided to give Christopher a 'holiday' from his school work. Special activities were organized over a two-week period, activities that Christopher was known to enjoy. This lifted his mood, decreased aggression, enabling him to get back into his work and school and be more accepting of his baby sister.

Access to psychological therapies

GENERAL PRINCIPLES

People who attract autism labels are seen as suitable candidates for many forms of therapy – for example, music, art, dance, psychoanalytic psychotherapy, counselling, play therapy, cognitive therapy, cranial osteopathy, swimming with dolphins. Different therapies have different aims and it is important not to mistake therapy for education. No form of therapy is appropriate to everyone with the label autism. There is simply not an adequate amount of research to enable us to judge who (if anyone) benefits from what. We still have a lot to learn and care is needed when making these decisions. It is wrong to waste resources on interventions which do not help; it is equally wrong to exclude people from interventions that may help them just because we do not like that particular approach. What can be stated with certainty is that the contribution of any individual therapy is tiny in comparison to the contribution of quality of life. Therapy may have a small but significant effect and as part of an overall approach can have a role to play. But life is the real healer, the real arena where change occurs. Therapy is no substitute.

Rather than trying to review all the many therapies on offer, we will focus here on how to decide whether a particular therapy is worth pursuing as part of the support for an individual. If you are thinking about the relevance of a particular form of therapy

- Try to get up-to-date information on what is involved and what current research there is (the autistic societies in a number of countries often do a good job providing this kind of information).

- Think of the goals that it is hoped to achieve and what other options there are for achieving those goals.

- Identify anything that will be given up if a particular approach is pursued.

- Talk things over with a trusted professional who is not going to be judgemental about your ideas.

- Work out how to evaluate as objectively as possible whether the therapy helps or not.

- Involve the person with autism as much as you possibly can in this decision making.

(C) Quality of social support

This issue is more fully dealt with in Chapter 5. It is mentioned here because it is vital to stress that the well being of the individual cannot be considered in isolation from the network of social supports in which the individual is embedded. High-quality relationships impact upon physical health, emotional well being, problem solving and self-esteem. Individuals need around them people who think well of them, respect them, like them and have a sense of humour. Not everyone that the individual comes across has to be like this. Rather, when you survey the people who are important in the individual's life, the majority should have one or more of these positive contributions.

(D) Quality of activities

The well being and self-esteem of the individual is likewise nourished by the activities in which he engages. This involves a number of key components. A lifestyle supporting well being will be one that is built around strengths and preferences, that delivers success and enjoyment. Well being cannot be sustained in a life made up predominantly of disliked activities, lack of pleasure and repeated failure. There is also a more subtle element to quality of activities. Human beings appear to do better when in the pattern of their life they can occupy a number of roles – be a friend, a helper, a worker, a partner, a supporter, a relative, a learner, a dependent, a leader, a follower. It is not clear how many roles over what time period are needed to experience well being. This is not an area that can be reduced to numbers. However humans may not do well when their life is made up over long periods of time of just one or two roles – son or daughter, learner, dependent. This is of course exactly what happens to many people who are identified as disabled. Therefore working to enhance quality of life means working to increase the number of roles that a person can fill, especially those that earn the respect of others in our present society (hence the importance of real employment, for example).

Finally there are two other components to quality of activities. One is pace of life. Some people function better with a lot of things happening, frequent changes and variety. Others function better when the pace is more measured. The second component is structure of life. Some people do better when life is well organized and predictable. This will be true for many people with the label autism (see Chapters 1 and 4). However others may function better with a more spontaneous kind of life. We need to be open to individual differences and not fall into autism stereotypes.

> *A residential home for people with autism changed its regime to offer a highly structured approach to daytime activities. Two brothers living at the home, who had hitherto participated in the more relaxed lifestyle of the home, took to their beds and refused to participate in this new structured and predictable life. So the home worked out how to operate in two ways – a very structured lifestyle for the majority and a more spontaneous (what-shall-we-do-today) approach for the brothers.*

The emphasis on quality of life requires a shift in how we think about supporting people. It means moving from fitting people to available services to building supports for the person to develop a life of her own. It means a change from a focus on professionally perceived needs to a focus upon the preferences of the individual. It means a focus on strengths not deficits. It means challenging the notion of readiness – people with disabilities, especially adults, are always being got ready for a life that never seems to arrive. The shift is to get a life…*now!* Many service planning systems are not adapted to this shift in perspective. Services may find it helpful to move over to the use of one of the person-centred planning systems (see Bibliography) to replace the more traditional individual planning systems. No system is guaranteed to deliver the outcomes that we are emphasizing. The real changes needed are in attitudes, in the hearts and minds of those supporting the person with the disability labels. However a system of work can support the change of perspective and make it easier to train new people in the approach required.

Concluding remarks

Enhancing and sustaining well being is about promoting the best quality of life possible for the individual. It is vital not to define loss or lack of well being as an individual problem which is addressed by 'fixing' the individual or providing individual therapy without consideration of the life that the individual is leading. Significant lifestyle interventions may be needed. However, these should be complemented by the smaller everyday interventions that influence personal well being, interventions that have been the focus of much of this chapter. It is not an either…or. Every little bit helps for people who are struggling to maintain or regain a sense of well being.

CHAPTER 7

Competence

What this chapter is about

One of the key resources that enables people to function constructively
in life is personal competence – the possession of knowledge and skills.
Lack of knowledge and skills in key areas is a major factor predisposing
to behaving in ways that others find challenging. This chapter is about
the ways in which behaviour is linked to lack of knowledge or skills;
and how interventions to enhance competence play an important role
in the support to people whose behaviour gives rise to concern.
Particular attention is drawn to:

- Knowledge about other people (their thoughts, feelings,
  perspectives) and the skills for interacting successfully with
  others.

- Knowledge about one's own feelings and thoughts and the
  skills for managing strong feelings.

- Knowledge about the rules of communication and the skills for
  effective communication.

- Specific skills, a lack of which may be very directly linked to
  the behaviour of concern.

- Discrimination and generalization of skills, which is another
  important area where lack of appropriate skills and knowledge
  can predispose to behaving in ways that others find challenging.

Most of these are areas of great personal challenge for people with
autism.

How lack of competence relates to behavioural difficulties

There are a number of ways in which competence (knowledge and skills) in the areas listed above relates to behavioural difficulties.

Social knowledge

One of the key resources that enables us to function in socially appropriate ways is the ability to see things from the point of view of other people. This includes awareness of how our behaviour might make others feel. Such thoughts as 'If I do this what will people think of me', 'How would I feel if this was done to me' and linked principles such as 'Do unto others as you would have done unto yourself' speak to this issue. Without these kinds of knowledge and understanding there is little to inhibit immediate impulses – to hit out because you cannot have what you want; to scratch someone because you enjoy the sight of blood; to take without paying for an item from a shop; to comment publicly upon someone's physical peculiarities; to demand that the person you like spends all her time with you...

Understanding rules of communication

Effective communication involves not just skills but also knowledge of certain important things. The person needs to understand that communication is an interaction between two or more people, that communication occurs because the listener has a mind and feelings that are different from his own and can be influenced by the process of communication. Without this understanding the person may not see the point of sharing information – the other should know already because the person himself knows. The person may not ask for the things that he needs – because he does not understand that his communication can directly influence the behaviour of others. It will be difficult to maintain joint focus – the person may burden the listener with vast amounts of redundant information, not knowing that the other already knows this information. He may switch topics without any explanation, assuming that the other understands the new topic being discussed.

Understanding one's own internal states

The relationship between moods, well being and behaviour is explored in Chapter 6. Many of our behaviours are directed towards maintaining internal equilibrium and to returning our internal state to equilibrium when equilibrium is lost – taking a tablet to relieve pain; going to bed early to relieve tiredness; eating to relieve hunger; calming ourselves if we are over-excited or angry; cheering ourselves up if we are feeling miserable. Such restorative actions are learned. However, the successful use of appropriate restorative actions depends upon our recognizing in the first place the physical or emotional state that we might find ourselves in. If a person does not recognize or understand the internal state, he will not know that action can be taken to relieve it nor does he know what action to take. Thus a pain may go unnoticed and unreported and develop into a serious physical problem; low mood or heightened arousal may not be understood and may escalate out of control.

Social skills

People who lack social skills are easily rejected by others. People with autism have great difficulties in the area of social skills. They may sometimes appear rude or intimidating in their interactions. They may avoid eye contact or may gaze with a continual stare. They may not know how to initiate conversations or social contact except through endless questioning, extensive monologues or behaviours which others find challenging (head banging, grabbing or screaming). Interactions may be terminated abruptly before the other has had a chance to respond. Not knowing how to join an ongoing conversation the person may butt in, talk across other people or place herself in between people already conversing. Ignorant of the rules about personal space and personal boundaries the individual may stand inches from the other, touch the other inappropriately, try to smell the other's hair. Strangers may not be discriminated from friends, so the interaction may seem quite inappropriate. Lacking knowledge about social norms, the person may not know how to ask for things in shops, how to wait in queues. Problems generated by this lack of social skills are compounded when others misinterpret the behaviour in question. Thus a large male who likes to talk to females but stands only inches from them may be interpreted as threatening (resulting in the female becoming anxious in his presence) or rude (resulting in the person being admonished or corrected). Either way a sequence of events may be set off, the final outcome of which is a behavioural incident. Lack of social skills may contribute greatly to the social isolation of people regarded as autistic (see Chapter 5).

Communication skills

When we have a strong desire or need then we experience discomfort until that wish or need is fulfilled or we have got used to the discomfort (which takes time and does not always happen). If someone else can sort out the problem, they may need to be persuaded to do so. If a person lacks formal communication skills, he may use a 'direct action' approach. For example, if the person wants to get out of the supermarket and starts shouting, screaming, pushing people and pulling people's hair, he finds that he is supported in leaving the supermarket quite quickly. Whilst this approach works for the person, it is challenging for others. Thus lack of communication skills sets a person up to solve problems in ways that other people may well define as problematic...especially when lack of communication is combined with lack of social understanding.

Arousal management skills

We all have the experience of social behaviour going astray when we become very emotionally aroused. We may become so manic and excited that we lose our social inhibitions and do things that others disapprove of – shouting, laughing hysterically, food fights...decency forbids us to go further! We may get so angry and frustrated that we lose control – scream, smash things, hit out, bang our head. Extremes of arousal lead to disinhibition – a threshold is passed and certain behaviours are released (see Chapter 3). Thus a key skill is to be able to monitor our own arousal and implement arousal reduction techniques as we approach the threshold – know when it is time to walk away, to go and take some quiet time to ourselves, take a few deep breaths, count to 10, put on some soothing music, go for a long walk or work out in the gym, go and play on the computer. The options are many but the skills of monitoring arousal levels and implementing arousal reduction strategies are essential. Without them loss of control becomes much more likely.

Specific coping skills

In addition to the more general skills and competencies discussed above there is a specific category of skills which may link directly to behaviour – skills which could achieve for the person a socially appropriate outcome which is currently being achieved through socially inappropriate means (this is the notion of functional equivalence). Thus a person who lacks verbal or gestural communication, and who does not want to perform an activity which he has been asked to do, may bite the person making the request as a way of communicating his message. A person may enjoy sensory pleasure (smells and textures) and finds ready access to the pleasures in his own bodily products. A person may like to be active but lacks skills to occupy herself – so she spends all day following her carer, who is a source of much stimulation and occupation. The challenge here is to teach the person alternative social, communication or self-occupation skills which would achieve similar results for her without the same dire social consequences.

Discrimination and generalization in learning

Problems can arise not because the individual lacks relevant skills but because he has not mastered fully the situations in which it is appropriate to use these skills – the rules that determine when, where, with whom, how often a skill should be used. This area presents particular challenges for people identified as autistic. Thus, behaviours sometimes become problematic, not because they occur but because the individual has not learned the boundaries within which the behaviour is appropriate or acceptable. This is a problem of discrimination.

- ○ Urinating is good…in the toilet, but not in the bedroom or garden.
- ○ Initiating conversations is excellent…with people you know but not with strangers in the street.

- ○ Masturbation is OK…in the privacy of your bedroom but not in public.
- ○ Helping yourself to food is appropriate…from the refrigerator in the kitchen but not from the shop without paying.
- ○ Clearing up after the meal is helpful…but when everyone has finished eating, not just when you have finished.

Alternatively a behaviour can become problematic because the person has not been able to transfer her skills outside of the learning environment and the skill has not become functional. This is a problem of generalization.

- ○ It is good to urinate in the toilet…but any toilet will do, not just the upstairs toilet in your home.
- ○ It is good that you do not bang your head when Bill is with you…it would be better if you could control this behaviour regardless of who is with you.

In all the above situations, behaviours which are otherwise appropriate are problematic because they occur too freely or too narrowly. The issue is to bring the behaviour under the control of cues that are 'appropriate'.

Strategies for building competence

Building competence, as the previous section suggests, is a complex and long-term endeavour. There are general skills and knowledge which need to be promoted and there are specific skills which a particular individual may need to learn in order to enhance her ability to cope with life's pressures. As well as the skills themselves, attention needs to be paid to their appropriate generalization and discrimination, so that they become truly functional for the individual.

Developing social knowledge

GENERAL PRINCIPLES

It is important to immerse the person long term in social knowledge development A key part of whatever 'curriculum' underpins our support efforts must be a drive to impart knowledge of self and knowledge of others – knowledge about one's own thoughts and feelings and about the feelings and thoughts of others. This should feature in everyday interactions and over very long periods of time. There are a number of components to this work:

- *Modelling.* Those who support the person will need to draw attention to their own feeling states and the events that contributed to these feeling states. They need to model the use of problem solving around day-to-day issues.

- *Concreteness.* When building links between events and feelings, the more visible and explicit the links are made the greater the chance for understanding to develop.

- *Feedback.* Those who support the person will need to feed back to him visible feeling states that the person is experiencing and, if known, the events connecting to those states.

- *Self-monitoring.* As well as immediate feedback we need to support people over time to develop systems for monitoring their feelings and actions (positive, not just negative).

TIPS AND HINTS

(1) Model on a day-to-day basis and in exaggerated form key emotions such as happiness, excitement, anxiety and anger. Draw attention to important face and body cues ('I'm smiling because I'm happy', 'I'm yawning because I'm tired'). State clearly how these emotions are influenced ('I'm feeling very happy because you helped me make the breakfast', 'I'm feeling angry because I've lost my pen').

(2) Use a set format with explicit language to model the process of solving day to day problems:

- What is it I have to do here?

- What are some ways I can do it?

- What will happen if I try this way? What will happen if I try this other way?

- How did my approach work?

- What should I do next time I have this problem?

(3) Spell out what you are thinking that might influence your upcoming behaviour. For example, something you have to do next means you need to finish the ongoing conversation.

(4) When teaching about feelings, use words that people themselves have already come up with (for example 'fizzy') rather than imposing a standard feeling vocabulary (such as happy, sad, anxious).

(5) Feed back on a day-to-day basis to people their reaction to particular events – label their emotions for them, explain why they may be feeling a particular way. (For example, 'You're laughing, you look very happy – is it because we are going to the park?') Explore the use of additional media – mirrors, photographs and video recordings of the individual engaging in activities which depict a range of their emotions. Review these regularly with the person. Build such review work into the ongoing routines.

(6) Make as concrete as possible the connections between behaviours and their consequences (for example, falling over connects to hurt, biting people connects to hurt, hurt connects to tears; buying nice things connects to money, breaking things connects to money being taken away).

(7) Use drama games and movement activities such as yoga, ballet or Sherbourne movement exercises to help build awareness of self and develop some idea about control.

(8) Use drama to help the person make a distinction between fantasy and reality, which may be a particular need for some.

(9) Use a range of teaching approaches to stimulate social thinking. Howlin *et al.*'s book (1999) describes a structured approach to teaching about emotions and about social perspective. Such teaching can also be carried out on an informal level, using every day opportunities – discussing what gifts someone might like for their birthday or Christmas; what is the thing to do if someone that you know

is upset or ill; how can you help someone who cannot do something; what would be a good surprise for someone.

(10) Develop classroom projects around specific emotions. For example, this month's project is 'sad'. We practise sad faces; collect pictures of sad faces; read stories about things that make people sad; discuss what makes us and others that we know sad; discuss what we should do when we feel sad and how to respond to others who are sad. Use a variety of media – writing, drawing pictures, role playing and drama, reading, analyzing TV soaps. Tony Attwood's excellent book on Asperger's Syndrome (1997) details a lot of these sorts of games and exercises.

(11) Use visual aids to help with monitoring feelings (for example line drawings of different facial expressions); and to develop understanding of strength of feeling (balloons of different sizes, bottles with different numbers of bubbles, mountains of different sizes).

(12) Develop scripts and stories around social situations that give different perspectives and ideas for positive action. The social stories work developed by Carol Gray (1994b) is an excellent example of the kind of work that we are talking about. She provides a format for developing short individualized stories, using specific types of sentences – descriptive, perspective and directive sentences – used in a particular ratio; the language is literal and the stories include positive action statements. The advantage of this approach is that it forces us to think very clearly about the core social messages that need to be communicated. The stories are presented in written or other visual format which is an easier medium for the person with autism. Having the story written means greater consistency between those supporting the individual.

Linda would become very anxious when she felt that someone was looking at her. In school, she would shout at her teachers to stop looking at her and temper tantrums were frequent. The following story was developed in order to help Linda understand about the importance of looking. 'When I am in school, my teachers often look at me. They look at all the kids. They look at us for many reasons. Sometimes they look to see if we are safe. Sometimes they look to see if we need help. Sometimes they look because we are doing something clever or interesting. Sometimes they look because they think we want to say something. Looking is part of their job, it is very important. I will try to remember that looking is important and good. I will try to smile when my teachers look at me.' It took just a few days for Linda to start to respond with a smile when her teachers looked at her.

(13) Use visual aids (pictures, cartoons) to portray other people's thoughts. This may make it easier for the person to grasp how what is in one person's head is not necessarily the same as what is in another person's head. Again, Carol Gray (1994a) has developed an excellent approach to this through the use of comic strip conversations. She uses simple line drawings of people, speech bubbles and thought bubbles to show how people in the same situation may have different thoughts and feelings and therefore act differently. She uses colour to depict different emotions. The person and his carers practise 'drawing' their conversations. The main points are drawn as the conversation takes place and the person is encouraged to think about what was said and the thoughts behind the words. The words and thoughts are written in different colours according to the emotions involved. Using this visual format helps the person to think about other people's perspectives and motives and to problem solve around difficult social situations which have occurred.

Teaching social skills

GENERAL PRINCIPLES

Social skill teaching takes place at both the formal and the informal level. It is important to focus upon the skills that the person needs now in his immediate social world and not on skills that might be of some use in the future. It is important to note also that an early start is helpful. It may be tempting not to correct socially inappropriate behaviours when children are young. For example, if a child has had difficulty communicating, parents may be so relieved when speech develops that they do not mind if she interrupts any conversation that they may be having with someone else. If a child has had difficulty approaching people, carers may be relieved when she starts to initiate approaches, even if these involve pinching or hair pulling. However, the longer such inappropriate skills are left to develop the harder it will be to teach appropriate skills at a later date.

Social skills should be modelled and directly shaped. They should ideally be taught in the environment in which they need to occur, although this is not always feasible – there may be practical difficulties, situations may occur too infrequently resulting in few opportunities for practice. Practice is essential and most skills need to be repeated many times over in order for them to become fluent. There remains a role for more structured and artificial skill teaching programmes. However, planning is required to ensure that the skills carry over to the natural environment – spontaneous generalization is unlikely and should never be assumed.

TIPS AND HINTS

(1) Teach specific social skills and clear behavioural rules for specific social situations (see also Chapter 5). For example: When you wish to speak to the teacher in class you must: put your hand up; remain silent until she asks you to speak or asks what you want; put your hand down; speak to the teacher.

- Use role-play to get the person to practise using the rules.

- Provide visual supports (written or drawn) to act as a reminder in the natural setting.

- A script or story may be helpful to explain why it is important to act in the way described.

- Initially the rules should be explained daily and role-played regularly (preferably just prior to the session in which they are to be used) until the person has learned and is using the rule.

(2) TV soaps can be useful as a means of teaching both social understanding and social skills – but great care is needed, as a large number of inappropriate behaviours can also be demonstrated on TV soaps.

(3) A formal social skills programme can be developed. The group should be small and involve people who are at a roughly similar stage in their development. Use at least two facilitators. The 'programme' is drawn up around the social difficulties that group participants experience. Common basic topics tend to be skills of relating (body language, conversations, listening), community living skills (asking, waiting, queuing, paying) and arousal management skills (keeping calm when something does not go according to plan).

- Social skills programmes should follow a predictable structure. This might include greeting, reviewing skills taught in the previous session and any homework assignments, introducing the new topic (role-playing appropriate and inappropriate responses and following a discussion, role-playing again the appropriate responses with all group members practising). Homework exercises can be set before the group closes and there should be a closing ritual.

- When running a social skills programme, each participant should have an individual folder, where written summaries of each session are kept (supported by other visual material) so that a permanent record is made which can be very useful for future reference.

- An effective social skills programme will take place as much in the real world as it will in the classroom. Always follow up teaching/role-play sessions with practice in real situations.

(4) Post visual reminders of key behavioural rules (do's and don'ts) – writing, pictures, cartoons – in the person's important environments. Separate visually the do's and don'ts. If the person is willing give her a set to carry around.

Teaching communication skills

A vast amount has been written about teaching communication skills for people with autism. We would encourage those who support people with the label to become as familiar as possible with this literature. Some useful references are included in the Bibliography. In the context of this book we cannot do justice to this large and complex topic and we are confining ourselves to a very limited number of general comments here. The section on teaching functionally equivalent skills (below) discusses the teaching of specific communication (and other) skills which are particularly relevant to the problematic behaviour that a person may show.

In the early stages of development it is important to build communication around the issues that are central to the individual. People need first and foremost to communicate about the issues that have real significance for themselves. If life revolves around food, spinning objects and avoiding certain colours, then the person needs to learn how to communicate about these things. Communicating about the toilet and saying 'please' and 'thank you' are unlikely to be high on the individual's agenda, though they may be high on ours. It is important always to start with the individual's agenda before going on to our own.

It is important to be very flexible about the method of communication that the person works with. We should not hesitate to use multiple forms. Many people identified as autistic will learn to speak. But not all. Others may need to develop alternative media – signing, using pictures, writing, using a keyboard, using other electronic aids. Even those who speak may find they can communicate more effectively by supplementing their speech with, for example, writing. We need to be tolerant of these individual differences and recognize that we are not yet able to pinpoint with any accuracy which medium will work best for each individual. That is why it is important in the early stages to use multiple media to communicate with the person and to let the individual try using different media himself (pictures, signs, written words) to see if he works more readily with one than another. This should become clearer during the course of the person's development.

When using alternative communication systems, two things need to be borne in mind. The communication system must be easy for everyone to 'read'. Speech, pictures and writing are easily understood whilst signing is less easily understood by the general public. The system should be capable of gaining the attention of others who may not be attending at the point of communication. Speech, electronic aids that synthesize speech and picture exchange systems do well on this count.

Speech is always to be preferred but is not feasible or very functional for some. There is no evidence that the development of speech is inhibited if multiple media are used. This is not surprising. Speech is such an effective and efficient tool in our society that if it can be developed it is bound to be shaped up.

Teaching functionally equivalent skills

GENERAL PRINCIPLES

Problematic behaviours reveal very clearly the things that are of central concern to the individual. When a particular behaviour is causing concern, it is necessary to assess what it is the behaviour is achieving for the individual, then to establish whether the person has a more appropriate skill they could use to achieve the same outcome. If they do not, we need to teach a socially appropriate and functionally equivalent skill. Teaching functionally equivalent skills is a powerful, well researched approach to reducing inappropriate behaviour (see Reference list). It depends for its effectiveness upon good quality functional analysis. We have not devoted space in this book to a detailed discussion of behavioural assessment techniques because not all the relevant behavioural needs of people with the label autism will be illuminated by such an assessment. There are many texts which deal with the specifics of assessment techniques and some of these are indicated in the Bibliography (see especially O'Neill et al. (1997)). In relation to developing relevant alternative skills a functional analysis of the behaviour of concern has a key role in deciding which skills to develop.

A functional analysis will show what it is that the behaviour achieves for the person – does it lead to getting something that is important (time with a favoured person, access to a quiet place, a break from work, access to a desired activity, exciting stimulation, food or drink)? Does it lead to avoiding or getting out of something unpleasant or unwanted (an uncomfortable place, people being too close, pain or discomfort, a difficult task)? The assessment process needs to pinpoint with precision what the behaviour achieves (it may be more than one thing) and then the person can be taught another way of achieving this same outcome. By and large this will mean teaching a specific comm-unication skill or skills, but not in every case. Sometimes it will mean teaching a leisure or self-occupation skill, such as how to do something interesting when there is no structured activity available...something that is just as interesting as breaking glass or poking a finger in behind the eye.

Teaching functionally equivalent skills is an approach which takes time to develop. Skills may take time to learn and to become useful on a day-to-day basis. Whilst not a quick fix, functional equivalence is a very powerful long-term strategy and therefore an important one to pri-oritize. As with all skill teaching, once the target skill is identified and broken down it needs to be taught in a way that makes it an effective alternative to the current behaviour. After all, from the individual's point of view, there is not much of a problem – he already has an effective way of getting his needs met. This means that any new skill being taught must also be effective. Thus it needs to be reinforced immediately, powerfully and every time. It must also be efficient. It therefore needs to be practised endlessly – drilled over and over – so that it becomes fluent and effortless. When it is more effective and more efficient it is at a point where it becomes a viable replacement for the problematic behaviour.

TIPS AND HINTS

(1) When a communication goal is identified to replace a behaviour of concern, make that a very long-term part of the person's individual plan...it should remain part of the plan even after the skill is achieved because of the risk of slipping back into old ways.

(2) Quite a lot of problem behaviours are a way of saying 'No...I don't want to do this'. The fear is that if you teach someone that it is OK to say no, they will say no to everything! Even if this were to happen it is not a major issue. If a person masters the skill of communicating 'No' by signing or pointing to a symbol or activating a device and this stops the behaviour that has been causing concern, that is to be celebrated. Once he is confident using the alternative, it then becomes a matter of gradually introducing some limits – for example, introducing a short delay before going along with the request (just finish this bit, a few more seconds) and then building on the delay time. Alternatively, work on discriminating between what is a choice and what is not. Use visual symbols to distinguish the two, and then gradually build up to a normal balance between rights and responsibilities.

(3) When teaching a functionally equivalent skill, ensure that in the early stages the behaviour is rewarded by achieving its intended outcome on each occasion and immediately.

(4) In the initial stages of teaching consider using artificial drill sessions to make the behaviour fluent.

Teaching arousal management

GENERAL PRINCIPLES

Assessment or observation of the individual's behaviour may highlight the role of arousal (excitement, agitation, anxiety) in behavioural events. If outbursts are shown to be linked to heightened arousal, the individual can be supported in managing this. The first strategy is to help the person to learn to monitor his arousal level. From this a scale can be developed to grade the level of arousal. A de-arousal skill can then be taught to use when a certain point on the scale is reached or the person can be encouraged to use a calming skill that she already has but rarely uses. There is more on this topic in Chapter 6. Finally, as with all skill teaching, the importance of role modelling must not be underestimated. We need to demonstrate on a day-to-day basis, through our own behaviours, how feelings can be dealt with in constructive ways.

(1) In everyday situations express clearly key emotions and
      demonstrate constructive ways of dealing with these. For
      example, 'I feel really angry because I lost my keys. I need to
      take some deep breaths and count to five. That's better, I feel
      calmer now'.

(2) The simplest way to begin teaching the individual about
      arousal level is to consistently label high and low arousal
      states as they naturally occur (you're uptight, you're stressed:
      you're breathing slowly and seem relaxed), so that the person
      learns to associate the feelings with a specific word or phrase.
      Incorporate any words that the person herself uses to describe
      such arousal states and never use 'good' or 'bad' around such
      states.

(3) For some individuals, it might be appropriate to feed back to
      them (verbally, using a mirror, using a Polaroid camera)
      variations in arousal that you can recognize in them. For some
      the use of physiology monitors may be helpful (t-shirts or
      rings that change colour as surface temperature changes,
      biofeedback equipment). For others role-playing can be used
      to raise awareness of how arousal levels are revealed.

(4) Use relaxation sessions to teach the experience of low arousal
      (see Chapter 6).

(5) Visual scales can be developed (using 3–9 points) to help the
      person rate the degree of arousal. These scales can be used on
      a routine basis to check arousal levels at various points in the
      day. It may be helpful to find an interesting visual
      representation of degree of arousal (for example, balloons of
      different sizes, arousal 'thermometers' or 'speedometers').

(6) Teach or encourage the use of a de-arousal skill when a
      certain point on the scale is reached. Key natural de-arousers
      include withdrawal to a quiet place, engaging in a repetitive
      but absorbing activity, music, walking, humour, engaging in a
      pleasurable though simple distracting activity. More
      professionalized approaches to arousal reduction usually

incorporate breathing exercises, muscular relaxation (see Chapter 6) and mental focusing (meditation).

(7) When teaching a new de-arousal skill, especially if it is hard to communicate effectively with the person about the whole concept, try and work within the person's own frame of reference. For example, if the person is calmed when she slaps her head then it may be easier to teach slapping of some other, less dangerous body area (for example chest and shoulders) than trying to teach a completely different calming technique such as slow breathing.

(8) A number of forms of self injury target body areas that have powerful points within the acupressure system. Teaching the individual to press or rub in these areas may support effective self-management in a non-dangerous way.

Teaching relevant discriminations

GENERAL PRINCIPLES

When a behaviour has become problematic because it occurs inappropriately – too often, in the wrong settings, at the wrong times, for too long, in inappropriate circumstances – then the conditions under which the behaviour is appropriate or acceptable need to be identified and this needs to be communicated to the individual. This can be done by ensuring that when the behaviour occurs in appropriate circumstances it is not interrupted (and therefore is likely to achieve a positive outcome for the person). However, when it occurs at others times the individual is interrupted and redirected to the appropriate circumstances (the room, the times, the materials). In this way the behaviour is not reinforced when it occurs inappropriately. If this approach is carried out consistently behaving under appropriate circumstances will be strengthened and behaving under circumstances deemed inappropriate will be weakened. Such learning is possible whether or not the person understands, at a more abstract level, social rules and the concept of 'appropriate'. Such learning is therefore accessible to all.

At the other end of the scale are the skills which are problematic because the circumstances under which they occur are very restricted. There is therefore a need to ensure that such skills are generalized to all the circumstances in which they are needed. Generalization should never be assumed. It sometimes needs to be painstakingly taught. The more restrictive the circumstance in which the original teaching takes places the greater the need to plan systematically for generalization.

TIPS AND HINTS

(1) One way to teach a discrimination is simply to state or demonstrate the rules under which the behaviour can be performed (for example, informing the person of the times at which they may talk about their special interest, of the place in which they can play their audiotapes).

(2) Complex discriminations may need to be simplified to make them 'accessible'.

Jeremy enjoyed spinning objects – any objects including crockery, cutlery, fruit, pens, electrical equipment. Spinning was his greatest pleasure. A strategy was developed whereby he was provided with a set of 'spinning toys', kept in a special bag and a fixed location. He was encouraged to go to his bag when he wanted to spin. If he tried to spin anything else he was immediately interrupted and redirected to his bag and given a lot of praise for his co-operation.

(3) Visual cues may be added in order to simplify a complex discrimination.

Wendy loved to tear paper. She would tear any form of paper – books, magazines, newspapers, toilet tissues, pictures. Her parents would give her old newspapers and magazines to tear but got upset when she tore up items not yet read or other valuable items. Wendy could not manage this discrimination. So her parents put a red sticker on the front cover of all materials that Wendy was allowed to tear. If she tore these – no problem. Attempts to tear anything else were quickly interrupted and redirected. It took time but Wendy eventually learned to discriminate.

(4) One way of teaching generalization is to get the individual to practise the behaviour with a range of relevant stimuli or across a number of relevant settings.

Ali went through an intensive toilet training programme at his school. He learned quickly but as soon as he arrived home he would be incontinent. Despite his parents' efforts, he would not use the toilet at home. It was only when his teacher came to the house and repeated the training procedure there that he began to use the toilet at home. His mother was involved in the training and the skill then transferred to his mother's requests. His mother in turn repeated the training procedure at the homes of Ali's grandparents and aunts and uncles. Generalization was effected but only in a rather painstaking way.

(5) Another way to facilitate generalization is to introduce gradually new elements into the situation.

Louise had one-to-one support at school and co-operated well with her support worker. However when the support worker was absent, no one could get Louise to co-operate with activities and tantrums were frequent. This was overcome with a detailed strategy. Each staff member in turn worked alongside the support worker with Louise. At first the staff member just shadowed (was present but did not intrude). The next step was for the staff member and support worker to alternate making requests. When this was successful the staff member took over more and more and the support worker faded back . . . literally, with her chair moving further and further so that Louise gradually came to co-operate with just the staff member. The whole process took several months. Once Louise could co-operate with all staff in the class, care was taken to rotate the staff working with her so that the generalization of co-operation was sustained.

Concluding remarks

Building competence is not a short-term remedy for behavioural difficulties. It is a central ingredient in long-term work. People with autism progress over time, more quickly in some areas than others. Progress is possible at any age. The things that we call impairments may just be things that take a lot longer to learn and sometimes we give up working on these things, particularly social understanding. It is hoped that this chapter will strengthen the resolve to persist even in areas where progress is hardest won.

CHAPTER 8

Obsessions

What this chapter is about

This chapter will look at behaviours which are often described as repetitive or obsessional. The person does the same thing over and over again. Sometimes the repetitive behaviour itself might be a problem – repetitively hitting other people hard on the back, repetitively stuffing toilet rolls down the toilet so that blockages and floods occur. Sometimes the behaviour itself is not so much of a problem but problems arise when any attempt is made to set limits on it – when you refuse to answer the same question again, when you try to stop the person spinning the crockery, when you try to stop the person going backwards and forwards through a doorway. The chapter will look at the different types of repetitive behaviour and what they mean. In particular distinctions will be made between special interests, compulsions and rituals. It will look at how these behaviours become implicated in significant challenges to others and at the various support strategies that follow from our understanding of these behaviours.

Breaking down the concept of obsession

The term 'obsession' is used rather loosely around people who have autism labels. It is applied to almost any repetitive behaviour. Yet there may be rather different motivations underlying such behaviours and this factor has very important implications for how we work with people around these issues.

One type of repetitive behaviour, often referred to as obsessional, would in other people be regarded as a hobby or special interest – something they would spend a lot more time on if they were free to do so. These are behaviours that are engaged in because they are positively reinforcing or generally pleasurable. Such behaviours can be many and varied – picking up all the leaves off the lawn, drinking tea, collecting bits of broken crockery, spinning objects, lining up chairs, reading about the private lives of the kings and queens of England. These are activities that the individual will happily spend time on and may get upset if the activity is prevented or interrupted.

A second type of repetitive behaviour is quite different in its motivational context. Here the behaviour is preceded by discomfort and the behaviour itself relieves that discomfort, albeit temporarily. Again, this type of repetitive behaviour is not unique to people with autism labels. Many people feel an overwhelming urge to engage in behaviours that are not really necessary or sensible (for example, frequently checking locks or gas taps, having to wash hands). The discomfort can be so strong that the individual experiences the behaviour to be beyond his personal control – hence the term compulsion. The forms that these behaviours take are varied – compulsions to touch people's eyelashes, tap others on the head, turn all light switches to the 'off' position, pull clothes off and then start to put them on and…pull them off and start again…and again…and again.

Exercise 8.1 Routines and Rituals

Divide a large sheet of paper into two columns, one narrow, one wide. The exercise is to list out your individual morning routine. In the narrow column put the times and in the wide column write out in detail what you do. Imagine that you need to inform a complete stranger of exactly what goes into making a 'good start' to the day for you.

When you have completed the list look at individual items and imagine if this did not happen or was prevented from happening – how would you feel?

The third type or repetitive behaviour is illustrated by Exercise 8.1, an exercise that Michael Smull uses to help develop more person centred thinking in how we support people (see Bibliography).

Human beings are incredibly ritualistic. We develop all sorts of behavioural sequences and arrangements that we like to be 'just so'. They seem to make life manageable and safe, give some sense of control and reflect important personal preferences. When these rituals are disrupted, discomfort is experienced and efforts are made to reinstate things to the way they 'ought' to be. Whilst we all have different rituals we often regard the rituals of other people as irrational.

Just like other people, people with autism have rituals that reflect how 'just so' they prefer things to be. Some of these behaviours, to which we refer as obsessional, may simply be the individual's preferred rituals.

Thus 'obsessions' are quite normal human phenomena. The differences in relation to people with autism are likely to be in:

○ The single mindedness with which they are pursued

○ The intensity of the personal experience

○ The lack of accommodation to the needs and views of others

○ The general lack of confinement to specific times, places and companions

○ The intrusiveness of the behaviours upon others

○ The extent to which the person is able to stop independently – the problem of perseveration or 'stuckness'.

The links between obsessions and behaviour

Obsessions involve very strong motivations and, for the person with autism, these are frequently associated with behaviours that are socially problematic. The strong desire to engage in the behaviour, coupled with a lack of social understanding about how that behaviour might affect other people, creates an outcome that others identify as challenging (for example, stuffing toilet rolls down the toilet pan is likely to result in toilet blockages or flooding; insisting that lights are always in the 'off' position causes irritation for others).

A second way in which problematic outcomes can be caused is where there is an inbuilt tendency to perseverate so that the person becomes literally 'stuck', unable to move on even though she may want to (she keeps washing her hands, the skin is raw and hurts but she can't stop herself and becomes more and more upset; the same thoughts keep going round in the mind and she cannot stop them so she keeps banging her head hard against the wall).

A third route to outcomes which others may find challenging is when the repetitive behaviour is combined with perfectionist tendencies. Frustration is created when perfection is not achieved – when things will not line up in exactly the right way, when people will not say exactly the words that they are supposed to say. The person becomes increasingly anxious and the attempts to achieve perfection become ever more intense.

Finally, and perhaps most commonly, problems arise when other people intervene to set limits on the behaviour in question: they stop the person taking all the batteries out of every device around, they refuse to discuss further who sang what song in what year, they say that 18 tea chests full of broken bits of china is enough, they say that the person has pulled their trousers up and down 30 times and that is enough. Such limit setting creates very strong feelings which may lead to general loss of behavioural control or more specific behaviours targeted at persuading the other to comply and to back off from trying to set limits.

Distinguishing between hobbies, rituals and compulsions

We have suggested that under the broad heading of obsessions are behaviours that vary somewhat in the motivations which are associated with them. Generally speaking, hobbies and special interests lead to positive reinforcement – they are engaged in because they achieve a positive outcome for the person. They may have a secondary effect of indirectly relieving stress that originates elsewhere (the person loves doing tapestry and also finds that it relaxes him after a difficult day; the person loves shredding paper and also finds it calms her when stressed).

At the other extreme, compulsions are generally about relieving discomfort which may be intense and there is a very direct link between the behaviour and the attempt to relieve the discomfort. There is a sense that the behaviour *must* be engaged in to relieve the discomfort…and only *this* behaviour will do, no other form of stress relief will be good enough. The relief will only be short term so that the behaviour will soon be repeated.

Rituals seem to have more mixed motivations. They probably arise to relieve strain on information processing – to avoid having to think through every situation. They may give a positive sense of control. It is good when things are 'just so' but it is also uncomfortable when things are not 'just so' and the person needs to make them 'just so' in order to relieve the discomfort.

The reason for making these distinctions between the various behaviours that may be labelled obsessional is a practical one. It is important to understand the motivational context for the repetitive behaviour of concern. This means carrying out a detailed functional analysis in order to pinpoint the motivation(s) underlying the be- haviour. As mentioned elsewhere functional analysis is not a topic which this book addresses in detail, as it is well covered in other texts. However, there are a few pointers, in addition to those mentioned above, to distinguishing particularly the two extremes – hobbies and compulsions:

- The accompanying signs of emotion will tend to be different. Hobbies and passions are generally associated with interest and delight, compulsions with tension or anxiety.

- Neither special interests nor compulsions show a very strong relation to attention from others (unless the behaviour itself requires a partner, as in verbal routines) or demands being made.

- Both may be much more likely at unstructured times, although the strength of this relation is likely to be more powerful for hobbies and passions than for compulsions.

- Compulsions are more likely to be accompanied by signs of general loss of well being and agitation and/or depression and to be linked to recurring cycles of altered mood states. Even for those who are more generally compulsive, the behaviours tend to become more intense and urgent when the person is agitated or depressed.

- ○ Special interests tend to be a longer-term, more continuous part of someone's functioning, rather than coming or going. They can, however, change in content, often quite dramatically.

- ○ Those experiencing compulsions will sometimes give evidence of trying to resist the behaviour – sitting on their hands, trying to physically contain themselves in other ways, saying over and over 'Don't ...'. This is less likely to be seen with passions or special interests.

Managing obsessions – general considerations

There are different approaches to dealing with special interests, rituals and compulsions. However there are some general issues to be considered in relation to constructive support around all repetitive behaviours.

(1) It is important to ask whether the behaviour itself poses a real problem. We may not share the interests that other people have, their rituals are not our rituals, what is a major issue for others may be of little concern to us. It is very important to go back to the points made in Chapters 2 and be clear as to whether the repetitive behaviour is levying or likely to levy costs upon the person or upon others; or is it just that *we* think that the behaviour is inappropriate and makes no sense and should stop. We have to think very carefully about whether we leave the behaviour alone or whether it is really to the person's advantage for limits to be set and the behaviours curtailed.

(2) It is important to be clear what the person would be doing instead if the repetitive behaviour ceased to occur or occurred less often. Any attempt to limit a highly probable and frequent behaviour is doomed to failure if it is not crystal clear what the person is supposed to do instead. There will be no success in just setting out to *stop* a behaviour. How will the person fill his time if unable to access his special hobby?

What is he supposed to do instead of…touching people's eyelashes, flushing clothes down the toilet?

(3)   We need to ensure that access to alternative behaviours is well structured. We have discussed already that many people with autism function better when activities are individualized, well planned, communicated and delivered consistently; and when the person is supported to engage in them; when there is a minimum of unstructured, undirected time. This is particularly needed when trying to set limits on high probability repetitive behaviours. A well structured life is a tremendous inhibitor for those with passions and compulsions. It holds them mentally and emotionally, providing focus, interest and distraction. It stops minds and behaviour wandering off. It stops anxiety overwhelming – it helps to keep in check the inner demons that otherwise would overwhelm.

(4)   We need to think about opening up new opportunities in the life of the person. Hobbies and passions usually reflect some exposure in life to materials, topics or situations which initially gave rise to the interest. Hobbies and passions can change. If we are unhappy with the present passion, we must make sure that the current lifestyle incorporates access to new activities which may trigger the hobbies or passions of the future. These of course may be equally challenging from our point of view as there is no way of predicting the specific interests that people may take up in the future.

Managing special interests (hobbies and passions)

GENERAL PRINCIPLES

First of all we need to celebrate people's interests. Having a special interest can be a tremendous asset, provided that it is not dangerous. For the individual it gives a sense of purpose in an often meaningless world; for supporters it relieves the pressure on always having to think up things to do – special interests are a great 'go to' option. For society it adds to the richness and diversity that make human beings so fascinating. Hobbies and interests can open up new roles and relationships for individuals. They can be the route to employment or other valued activities and thereby enhance self-esteem (the love of clocks – the horologist; the love of numbers – the accountant; the love of arrays – the shelf filler).

> *Angela loved to rummage in the dustbins. Rather than stop the behaviour, she was given the regular job of sorting the rubbish for recycling (bottles/paper/plastic) and ensuring rubbish was placed in the appropriate bins. Regular time was scheduled every day for this activity. A condition of this job was that she wear disposable gloves whilst sorting the rubbish and always wash her hands afterwards.*

Special interests can be used to expand the person's social circle by getting him involved with clubs for fellow hobbyists – photographers, ecologists, model makers, transport lovers.

> *Alan's passion for religion brought him into contact with the local church group. He became involved in a wide range of church activities which gave him a rich and fulfilling life.*

Special interests can enhance self-esteem by making the person a valued member of a group in other ways. A knowledge of 1960s music or soccer may give the person a place on the pub quiz team; a knowledge of countries and flags means that everyone is going to want the person on their team for the class geography quiz.

> *Max's passions were map reading and memorizing people's birthdays. He was given the job of route planning and navigating whenever outings were organized in his group home. He was also given the job of keeping track of birthdays for the people that he lived with and those who worked at the house. He would let the service manager know a week ahead of a birthday so that cards and gifts could be organized. Both these jobs raised his self-esteem by giving him a new and valued role in the home.*

Special interests can thus be viewed from the point of view of the opportunity that they offer for the individual to develop valued social roles. Linked to this, new skills can be developed around special interests.

Roy loved power plants. Using this interest he was helped to develop new knowledge in relation to science – and new social, literacy and planning skills (organizing a visit) plus new money skills (paying for the trip).

Almost by definition hobbies and passions are high probability behaviours. This means that they can be used to motivate and to reward. It is a lot easier to work on less favoured but important skills if such work is followed by access to an activity which is of major interest (such as extra time on the computer, extra newspapers to add to the pile.)

Finally it is important to recognize that these behaviours can take over a person, intrude unreasonably in the lives of others and create tremendous problems when attempts are made to set limits. There is no fundamental problem in limits being accepted. It depends upon how those limits are set and how committed the people without the hobby are in setting those limits. Limits should be set using clear, perceptible, consistent rules. This involves a number of steps.

(1) The nature of the limit needs to be decided with clear signals to indicate when the behaviour is allowed and when not. Limits need to be set in terms of:

- Frequency. *You can talk about winds and pylons 5 times a day for 15 minutes each time and somebody will be available to talk with you at these times. If you start to talk about these subjects outside of the allotted times you will be reminded when the next session is scheduled.*

- Duration. *You can flick leaves in the garden for 15 minutes. After 15 minutes a buzzer will sound and it will be time to come indoors.*

- Place. *You can only twiddle with your straws in the house. You must leave them in the bag by the door whenever we go out.*

- Materials. *You can only rip up the paper in your 'shredding box'.*

(2) If the behaviour is occurring most of the time, there will need to be very few limits to start with and then limits gradually increased until the hobby is occurring at a level which is defined as acceptable.

(3) Use visual signals to inform about the limits on the behaviour. *You can fill X number of boxes with your possessions; you can collect newspapers until the stack reaches the line on the wall; you can only spin the objects in the one 'hobby box'; I will only answer the question X times and I will check off on this sheet each time that I answer.*

(4) The limits need to be stuck to, kindly but firmly, even in the face of initial upset. But if something is promised or scheduled it must be delivered.

It is to be expected that limits set in this way will in time be tolerated but that the person with the interest will always try to push those limits and will usually succeed in getting one over on people without the interest. This is never an issue settled once and for all!

TIPS AND HINTS

(1) Check out your own feelings in relation to special interests to make sure that the reason for setting limits is that the behaviour is causing real problems rather than you thinking that it is a silly way to be spending time.

(2) Hobby boxes are very helpful for interests that involve doing something with specific items (flicking, spinning, juggling, dismantling, tearing). They have to be kept supplied and always accessible at the agreed times.

(3) Incorporate times for special interests into the visual schedules that you are using to get across to the person when, where and with whom important events occur.

(4) The most difficult problem in limiting hobbies is the problem that those setting the limits have in being consistent. Such inconsistency is confusing and handicapping for the person in need of support and can lead to angry confrontations. However, once the person finds out that you can be trusted and that she does get predictable access to her special interest the intensity subsides and the limits can be tolerated well.

(5) When setting limits, use a warning signal (a kitchen timer or analogue watch, for example) that gains the individual's

attention, to let him know that the activity is about to come
to an end (warning a few minutes before the end point). Let
the person know the next activity that he is to move on to.
Consider using a 'counting out' procedure as part of the
transition ritual.

(6) Get the person as involved as you can in deciding what the
limits will be (when and where the chat will take place, how
far up the wall to draw the line, how many times to repeat the
question, how long on the computer); and how they will be
enforced ('Do you want me to take the newspapers out or will
you? Do you want to be there or would you rather I took the
items out when you are not around?'). But once the rules are
set, stick with them.

(7) With repetitive questions it can help to write the answer for
the person after you have answered for the last agreed
time…the person can be redirected to the written answer
when they start the discussion outside of agreed times.

(8) Engaging in a special interest can be very calming. If the
individual's hobby has this effect try to schedule the hobby
for times of predictable stress or intervene early in the build
up of stress to divert the person. Try not to give access to the
special interest immediately after something unacceptable has
been done. This runs the risk of directly reinforcing
unacceptable behaviour.

Managing compulsions

GENERAL PRINCIPLES

For some people their compulsive behaviours are long-standing and
relatively invariant. It is what they always do when faced with a
particular opportunity or situation. More commonly, however, such
behaviours are associated with a loss of well being. This is particularly
likely when the repetitive behaviour appears to have escalated beyond
the person's control (for example, the person wants to eat, but cannot,
the need to do a particular behaviour gets in the way; the person does
not want to hit himself, but cannot help it) or if the behaviours have

become more intense and harder to break away from (for example, it is now taking three hours to get dressed instead of 15 minutes). The first priority in such instances is to boost the person's sense of well being (see Chapter 6). This may mean working on general quality of life and physical health, providing access to specific therapies and/or mood enhancing medications. When the person is experiencing a lowered sense of well being and the compulsions have 'taken over', it remains important to maintain some minimum level of demands on the person. He may not be able to tolerate as many demands as he did previously but it is not wise to withdraw all demands and leave the person to his own devices as this is likely to make matters worse, not better. Decide on the (fewer) demands that you will continue to make consistently – and do that.

It may be helpful to re-schedule activities in order to incorporate several relaxation/calming sessions into the day. The form that these take will depend to some extent upon the nature of the person's problems. For those with verbally expressed concerns, scheduling regular sessions during which the person may talk about his worries can diffuse the build up of emotion. For others, more direct forms of relaxation through sensory media such as music, massage, aroma, yoga or physical exercise will be more appropriate.

If the behaviour appears very dominant and out of the person's control it may be helpful to remove the things which trigger the compulsive act. For example, if decorations on walls and shelves are compulsively eaten, the walls and shelves may need to be stripped bare. If the presence of taps triggers compulsive drinking of water to the point of physical damage, a locking mechanism may need to be installed. If a particular staff member triggers compulsive aggression, that person may need to be removed from the support rota. These are difficult decisions that implicate legal and general human rights and great care is needed in making these decisions. However, it is sometimes the most appropriate thing to do. And, of course, it is a temporary alteration. These triggers can be gradually reintroduced once the person's well being improves and she is better able to develop tolerance.

It may be possible to help the person develop an effective inhibitory response – what to do with the hands or feet when he experiences an overwhelming urge to push or kick, what to do with his hands when he experiences an overwhelming urge to touch the eyelashes of everyone that passes in the street. This is likely to involve some trial and error. However, close observation of the individual will often reveal that he has already developed to some extent a strategy (a way of sitting or arranging the hands, for example) and this will be the best point to work from. If not, then the starting point will be to encourage a behaviour which is, literally, physically incompatible with the behaviour in question (for example, if the arms are folded tight or buried deep in pockets they cannot at the same time be slapping the face).

There is another difficult decision to be considered – a decision about whether it is worthwhile interfering in the compulsive act itself. Obviously if the person himself or others are being directly harmed or if she is experiencing increasing anxiety and distress as the behaviour continues, then we must intervene. Otherwise it is a judgement based upon detailed knowledge of the individual. It may be better to let the person dress in her own way, at her own pace, with all the checking and repeating because she gets there in the end and if you try to hurry her along or stop the repetitions this only makes matters worse. It may be better to let her rush over and smash three cups because that is all that happens but if we try to interfere somebody is likely to get hurt. On the other hand, we may know for another person that we can set limits on his behaviour and such limits are tolerated. Once a strategy is decided upon, consistency in implementation is essential.

Tackling the compulsive behaviour without tackling the mood disorder or physical health need is unlikely to be effective. As well being improves more systematic work can be undertaken. This may involve helping the person to take control over the compulsive behaviour by teaching or encouraging self-control or incompatible behaviours, gradually increasing exposure to the triggers for compulsive behaviours (see Chapter 9) or setting gradually tighter limits on the behaviour (for example, the number of repetitions, the amount of time allowed for the behaviour).

TIPS AND HINTS

(1) If possible, keep the person as involved as possible in making decisions about how she wants to be supported in limiting compulsions even when she is at a very low point. Make this a positive achievement – real courage and perseverance – get the person to monitor her successes. Remember, you're helping someone climb Everest – make it that way!

(2) Reinforce use of self-control strategies. Look for naturally occurring self-control tactics and support those. For example, provide clothes with deep pockets if that helps keep the hands and arms in check, provide a table and chair in a corner if sitting behind that table helps the person control rushing across the room to engage in the compulsion, cue supporters to step back when the person is sitting on their hands or backing against a wall if this signals that he is working hard not to grab glasses or poke eyes. Many people will use such self-control tactics, whether or not they can tell you verbally what they are doing.

Sam was experiencing an extended phase of agitation. His aggressive behaviours had escalated. He was particularly targeting two female staff members whom he liked enormously. He began to refuse to leave his room when he knew they would be around and if one of them was allocated to work with him, he would insist they stood at the far end of the room. If he had to pass by them, he would clasp his hands tightly behind his back. Initially these behaviours were perceived by staff as non-compliance and greater pressure was placed upon him to come out of his room and participate fully in all activities. This resulted in Sam becoming more distressed and much more aggressive. Once it was recognized that these behaviours were his attempts at controlling his own aggression, he was supported in using these tactics, with a resulting decrease in aggression and an improvement in his mood.

(3) Teach self-control behaviours. If the person has not developed any way of inhibiting his own behaviour, it may be helpful to teach him a self-control behaviour or strategy. Role-play can be a helpful teaching tool. The person should be reinforced

for using the self-control tactic in real situations. The reinforcer will need to be individually tailored to the likes and preferences of the individual. Self-control will take time to master and it is better to start with encouraging control in specific situations and for short periods of time and build up gradually rather than the person being expected to exert control in all situations at all times.

Linda had a compulsion to lash out at anyone who passed close by in the street. She was taught that when she was out, she should: look straight ahead of her, rather than at people who might be passing: keep her hands firmly in her pockets: tell herself 'It's OK, I'm doing well, I'm keeping my hands in my pockets'. The strategy was practised several times using role-play until she had learned it well. She went out initially for very short walks (no longer than 5 minutes) in order to practise self-control and was rewarded with a favourite activity when she succeeded. The time was gradually extended (to 7 minutes, then 10 minutes, then 15 minutes, etc.) as she became more confident.

(4) If the person is clearly stuck and cannot end the behaviour himself, you may need to step in and help.

Vance always had difficulty getting himself dressed. His clothes would be stripped off no sooner than he had put them on. It would normally take him 15 minutes to get his clothes on. However, during phases when his mood became depressed, it could take him four hours to get himself dressed. He would become more and more anxious. It was not helpful to allow him to carry on putting his clothes on and then taking them off. A limit was set – he was given 20 minutes to complete dressing. After 20 minutes a buzzer sounded and staff stepped in to help him put and keep his clothes on. When staff took over in this way, Vance's anxiety immediately reduced.

(5) When setting a limit, always give the person a warning about how much time they have left to continue with the behaviour before someone steps in to assist. Counting the person out may prove an effective transition ritual for some.

Managing rituals

GENERAL PRINCIPLES

The first question to ask is whether there is a problem. As we have already said, rituals are part of the human condition. One of the wondrous elements of human diversity is the range of habits and rituals that become important to individuals. There are individual differences in both the rituals that are important and the extent of ritualization (how many aspects of a person's life are affected). So, provided that the ritual is neither harmful nor unduly intrusive, we need to make reasonable accommodation. This may not be as simple as it seems. People with disability labels often have large numbers of people passing through their lives. If a ritual is being supported then all those who come into the person's life need to know about the routines that are to be respected.

If the ritual causes demonstrable harm to the person or to others or intrudes significantly, then rules may need be set around when, where, with what and under what circumstances the behaviour is acceptable. For example, it is acceptable to arrange the ornaments in your own room but not in shared spaces; you can be first in the queue in this situation but not that one; you can line chairs up but not if people are sitting on them; you can pick the grass from that area of the garden but not other areas; I will answer you five times but no more than that.

TIPS AND HINTS

(1) Reorient your service around person-centred planning (see Bibliography). This approach gives emphasis and respect to the importance of rituals.

(2) Give the person as much control as possible over limit setting. For example, get the person involved in drawing the lots that decide who goes first in the queue, get the person involved in which area of the garden they can pick grass from.

(3) Try and teach the person a disappointment routine – what to do when things are not 'just so'.

(4) Use social stories (see Chapter 7) to teach that a person's habits cannot be imposed on others (for example, just because

the person likes to be on time for work does not mean that he must tell off anyone else who comes in late).

(5) Get the individual to interview other people about their rituals to learn how people differ.

Concluding remarks

Repetitive behaviours are part of the human condition. We all have our individual special interests, not necessarily shared by others. We all develop rituals around certain daily activities. Some of us develop compulsive behaviours and obsessional thinking. Perhaps people with autism labels are more prone to these normal phenomena, perhaps not. What is certainly true is that, for people with autism, the behaviours may come to play a role that is significantly harmful to the person or to others. Nevertheless these behaviours are of great importance to the person – they provide joy, occupation, security and comfort, relief from stress. They can increase in frequency and intensity as the person's anxiety level increases, when mood becomes depressed or when the person feels unwell. They may be a sign to us that all is not right for the person. Intervening to stop the compulsive behaviour, break the routine or curtail engagement in the special interest can result in anger or distress. We hope that in this chapter we have been able to provide the reader with some useful ways of thinking about such behaviours and some strategies and tactics for intervening to limit them...when such interventions are justified.

CHAPTER 9

Sensitivities

What this chapter is about

This chapter is about the things that evoke discomfort, fear or other distress and about how these reactions play a role in behavioural difficulties. People with autism are often very sensitive to particular stimuli and events in their environment. Stimuli can be sensory experiences in almost any modality – sight, sound, touch, taste, smell. Sensitivity may be expressed as heightened awareness – the person picks up sounds that others cannot hear, the person sees particles of dust or dirt that others do not notice. It may be expressed as a reduced tolerance of particular stimuli – particular colours or patterns, anything which breaks up the smooth line of the walls (furniture, wash basins). Such reduced tolerance may spill over into an aversive reaction when the sensory stimulus creates physical distress – certain sounds are experienced as painful, certain types of light as uncomfortable, certain textures as intolerable. A second kind of sensitivity refers to a situation where an identifiable stimulus creates tremendous emotional distress – the sight of a dog, walking through a doorway, the close proximity of other people, making a mistake, having to wait. The third kind of sensitivity is expressed as worries. The person becomes preoccupied with certain topics which worry her – the effects of the weather on electricity pylons, the effects of rain on soil erosion. The thoughts dominate the person's life, they give little pleasure and they block the person's ability to engage in more positive behaviours and experiences.

The links between sensitivities and behaviour

The links between sensitivities and behaviour are likely to be direct although not always easily recognized by others. The distress caused by the sensitivity may be so extreme that it leads to loss of behavioural control. Thus, when the car pulls up at traffic lights the person gets so distressed that he attacks the driver; when he hears a sound which is painful to his ears, he gets so distressed that he bangs his head or bites his carer.

Alternatively, the distress caused may lead to the person taking control by initiating behaviours that will terminate the stimulus directly or get her out of the intolerable situation. Unable to tolerate people coughing, the individual hits offenders so that they tend not to cough around him in future; being very frightened of cats he runs in the opposite direction whenever one appears...but he lacks road sense; disliking disruption to the smooth lines of the wall, he destroys all the furniture in the room.

Worries are also a type of sensitivity. Certain topics preoccupy the individual and she spends a lot of time thinking and talking about the topic in question. Reassurance is constantly sought and she finds it difficult to focus on other things in life. Sometimes the thoughts can lead to increasing anxiety which, if not diffused, may lead to behaviour that others will find challenging. For example, she worries about what will happen if the bus is late and anxiety builds as she waits – if the bus is at all late, worry overwhelms her and she starts to shout and scream at the bus stop; because it is windy, she starts to think about hurricanes and people dying – she gets more and more worried until she goes to her room and smashes up all the furniture. Worries are often made worse when the person is overall in an anxious state.

If we know what concerns a person, the things that he is sensitive to or worry about, we can often support him in a way that reduces the anxiety and prevents loss of control. Problems can arise if we are unaware of the sensitivity. Thus, the child picks up the sound of a train operating some miles away. No one else notices. He becomes agitated and puts his fingers in his ears – and is told to put his hands down; he gets up to leave the room – and is told to sit down. Not long after he throws himself to the floor, shouting and screaming. The behaviour is described as 'out of the blue' and the child labelled 'unpredictable'.

Sensitivities can engage very strong emotions in the person and strong motivations to terminate the stimulus or event causing distress. The associated behaviours can be very problematic and are made more likely if the individual's sensitivities are not well understood by others.

Managing sensitivities

Providing reassurance and avoiding unnecessary exposure to the sensitivity

GENERAL PRINCIPLES

It is important that our processes of getting to know and understand the individual incorporate the identification of that person's sensitivities. This should be part of our general approach to support. It is particularly important if we are identifying behavioural incidents that appear to be triggered by nothing in particular. If behaviour appears 'out of the blue', then it is worthwhile exploring the possibility that a sensitivity is present of which we are unaware. Following from this, the individual is entitled to expect that anyone who supports her is fully aware of her sensitivities.

Knowing about a person's sensitivities enables us to look at how we can avoid exposure to the stimulus in question. After all, none of us deliberately exposes ourselves to the things to which we are sensitive without very good reason. It may be quite possible to do this without any major compromise on quality of life and without any unreasonable intrusions on the rights of others. If the person is sensitive to the noise of the vacuum cleaner or the lawn mower, then perhaps these activities can be done when the person is not around. If the doorbell sound causes distress, perhaps a knocker, a buzzer or an intercom would be easier to cope with. If chairs scraping on hard floors is a problem, rubber stoppers on the chair legs may help. Even if exposure cannot be avoided, it may be possible to reduce the impact of the sensitivity on the individual.

> *Alan continually worried about the whereabouts of everybody in the house where he lived (he shared this house with five other individuals). The worst times of day were mornings when people were leaving the home and the evenings when people started to return home again. He would become very distressed if he could not locate everyone in the*

house. By arranging for Alan to leave the house before everyone else in the morning and to return to the house after everyone else his anxiety at these times was greatly reduced.

Martha experienced phases of intense disturbance in her sense of well being. During these phases she was greatly troubled by decorative items on the wall and would seek to get rid of them by either eating them or flushing them down the toilet. During these periods, therefore, all decorations were removed from the wall until her sense of well being was improved and then they were gradually reintroduced into her environment.

When avoidance of the sensitivity is not possible and its impact cannot be reduced (for example, the noise level turned down) then reassurance becomes important. We need to convey to the person that we understand that he is distressed and, if we know, that we understand why he is distressed. It is important to convey that we do not see the distress as silly or unreasonable and that our concern is genuine. For some people the opportunity to talk about their sensitivity may be helpful. Distraction is always very important.

Avoidance and reassurance are key areas of support. Another may be the providing of information. The distress may be based upon a misinterpretation or misunderstanding of a particular circumstance – what is meant when someone looks at you, how the noise is caused, what different kinds of wind patterns there are. The work here is to expand the person's understanding and certainly to balance the emphasis on negative meanings with positive possibilities (looks may be friendly as well as hostile, rain helps things grow and get stronger and does not just wash things away).

Finally we need, once again, to pay close attention to the individual's overall well being. Sensitivities are much more unpleasant and tolerance much harder to manage if the person is stressed, depressed or unwell. Enhancing and maintaining well being (Chapter 6) therefore has a key role to play in this as in so many other areas.

TIPS AND HINTS

(1) Try making a video recording of the situations in which 'out of the blue' incidents are most likely to occur to see if you can pick up potential sensory sensitivities that are not apparent from ordinary observations.

(2) Try getting the person to wear a mini stereo to block out unpleasant sounds or sunglasses to block out bright light.

(3) Pay attention to décor and furnishings. Use soft lighting, pastel colours, plain wall and floor coverings. Use curtains and carpets to reduce noise levels.

(4) Support people to leave distressing situations – do not force them to remain in a situation that causes discomfort unless this is unavoidable or part of a plan based upon a careful assessment of the person's behaviour.

(5) Use scripts or social stories (see Chapter 7) to provide information about situations that cause distress. The information should be positively written, stating positive aspects of the situation and putting into perspective the negative aspects.

(6) For the person with good expressive language skills who has specific worries upon which he dwells, regular sessions in the day to discuss the worries may stop the person becoming overwhelmed by them. These sessions allow the person to be listened to carefully and permit problem solving around the worries themselves. The sessions should be limited in duration (agreed in advance) and follow a prearranged structure.

(7) If you note early that a child has a sensitivity to errors – cannot bear making mistakes or getting things wrong – go to work on it right away. This can become a surprisingly serious problem over time. Use social stories to explain that mistakes are all right, model making mistakes and using coping strategies, reward tolerance of less than perfect performance, teach a system for grading personal performance that is used over time and in a variety of domains.

Building tolerance of the things that disturb the person

GENERAL PRINCIPLES

There are two related approaches to building tolerance that have a wealth of research and experience behind them. The first is the principle of graded exposure. This teaches the individual tolerance of those stimuli or situations that it is thought to be reasonable to tolerate, by graded and controlled exposure to the triggering events. This means:

(1) Assessing the current level of tolerance for the situation – the person will sit for five seconds and no more; will tolerate a mattress in the bedroom but no furniture or pictures; will tolerate paper cups and plates but smash anything china that is on the table.

(2) Deciding the level of tolerance to be achieved – sitting for ten minutes; tolerating a bed and wardrobe in the room; using china cups and plates.

(3) Working from the current to the desired level, systematically and slowly, making only small changes as you move from one tolerance level to the next. Tolerance has to be stable at a level before moving on.

(4) Celebrating all achievements.

Angela lived at home with her parents. She would not tolerate any ornaments or pictures, not even the television, in the living room. The room was bare, except for a sofa and an empty bookcase. A graded approach was used to help Angela tolerate more things in the living room. Initially a small picture was hung on the wall in a corner of the living room, very high up and out of reach. When this was tolerated it was replaced with a slightly bigger one, a little lower on the wall. The next step was a second picture hung on another wall of the room. This process was continued (adding another item/waiting for tolerance to develop) until the living room was fully furnished. Each step took several weeks.

Gill would sit for a maximum of ten seconds before getting up to run around the room. The programme started with getting Gill to sit for seven seconds at a task (a buzzer signalled the end of the period) then rewarding her with a favourite piece of fruit and encouraging her to run around the room. After success was reliably achieved, the time was gradually extended, a few seconds at a time, until she was able to sit for several minutes.

A refinement of the graded approach to building tolerance is desensitization. This is particularly suited to situations when the intolerance is based upon anxiety, when it is (or is more like) a phobia. Desensitization is a carefully structured and well researched approach. It is carried out in controlled sessions and involves a number of key elements.

(1) Developing a hierarchy of situations around the specific sensitivity, organized from the least to the most uncomfortable. For example, a hierarchy for a fear of dogs might involve looking at cartoon drawings of dogs, looking at videos of dogs, looking at dogs through a window, seeing a dog on a lead far away, and so on.

(2) Teaching a relaxation response which works for the individual (taking deep breaths, engaging in a repetitive behaviour, listening to a favourite piece of music, eating a favourite fruit or snack, self-massage around key acupressure points) and which is used easily in everyday situations.

(3) Exposing the person with support to the least discomforting situation (in the above example, this might be to cartoon pictures of dogs). Relaxation is encouraged and exposure is ended before significant distress occurs. The person is reinforced for coping.

(4) Repeating the exposure with relaxation and reinforcement until the situation is well tolerated.

(5) Moving to the next step on the hierarchy (for example, watching a video of dogs) and repeating the process of exposure, relaxation and reinforcement.

(6) Setting each step so that there are only small increases in anxiety as you move from one step to the next. Desensitization avoids exposure to high levels of anxiety.

(7) Continuing in this way until the person can cope reliably with the situations in everyday life that cause significant distress.

Desensitization needs careful planning and implementation, and consumes a certain amount of time, although sessions themselves may only last 10–30 minutes. It can be a successful means of empowering coping.

TIPS AND HINTS

(1) Using favourite cartoon/fantasy characters can sometimes be a good way of getting someone to practise tolerance of uncomfortable situations (how would...respond in this situation).

(2) In desensitization sessions food is a great reinforcer – it encourages perseverance and eating also tends to inhibit anxiety.

(3) Get the person as involved as you can as an active participant in graded change and desensitization. These approaches can be effective for those people who find it hard to grasp what they are working on; it is easier if the person can actively participate and see what she is doing as a real achievement for herself and admirable in the eyes of others.

(4) Enlist significant others to admire and encourage what the person is working on.

(5) In desensitization, always be prepared to go back a step or even more, and repeat desensitization to earlier items in the hierarchy, should the person's anxiety increase during the work. Be prepared to add to the steps in the hierarchy if there are large increases in anxiety as you move from one step to the next.

Accessing specific therapies

GENERAL PRINCIPLES

There are a number of specific therapies which aim to reduce the discomfort caused by sensory-perceptual stimuli. Many of these are opposed by establishment professionals and bureaucracies, many are poorly researched, yet make great claims as to their impact upon the functioning and well being of people with autism.

Sensory Integration Therapy This was developed for children with sensory defensiveness (an excessive and negative reaction to ordinary sensory inputs), not all of whom are children with autism. The problem is seen as a difficulty in processing simultaneously and immediately the various sensory messages which arise when performing the simplest action. Its aim is to improve sensory awareness and the ability to respond simultaneously to several sources of sensory information. It involves a well structured set of exercises planned by a competent practitioner (usually an occupational therapist). The exercises involve a range of sensory stimuli such as swings, balls, brushes, materials of different textures, different aromas, lights, massage. It is relatively easy to implement and the approach has been used for a long time. Unfortunately the research studies carried out so far do not indicate that it has any specific effect although it is not known to cause harm either. It is an option to consider but it is worth trying to get an update on research findings before making a final decision.

Auditory Integration Therapy This is targeted specifically at discomfort caused by sound. It involves assessment by a trained practitioner for specific sound sensitivities. There follows a series of sessions at a specialist centre – usually 20 half-hour sessions over a period of 10 days. The sessions involve playing music through headphones. The particular sounds to which sensitivity has been identified are electronically filtered out, then gradually reintroduced. Great claims and great scepticism have surrounded this therapy. At the time of writing, current research suggests that some people with autism may benefit from sessions when music is played through headphones but the filtering process does not seem critical to this. There have been reports of negative side effects (increases in aggressive behaviours). Again, it is an option to consider but it is worth trying to get an update on research findings before making a final decision.

Scotopic Sensitivity Training This is not a specific therapy and was not developed exclusively for people with autism. It was developed for people who appear to have an abnormal sensitivity to certain wavelengths of light and involves the wearing of specially designed lenses. The lenses are of different colours, according to the individual's particular sensitivity. Some people with autism (notably Donna Williams (1992)) have found benefit from the use of these special (Irlen) lenses which seem to compensate for some of the visual discomforts. There seems to have been little systematic research in this area at the time of writing. The reader is encouraged to get an update on research findings before making any decision.

TIPS AND HINTS

(1) New therapies appear regularly. Before embarking on such therapies, it is important to look at the research findings to see what is known about

- What the therapy achieves

- For whom it achieves it

- Possible side effects – positive and negative

- Costs in terms of money, time and 'hassle'

- Other approaches that might achieve the same goal.

(2) The research database for many of the new therapies is scant and decisions often have to be made on the basis of limited information. So, when deciding upon an approach

- Be clear in your own mind what you want the approach to achieve

- Identify what will be different from how things are now, if the therapy works

- Measure the current situation and repeat these same measures during and after the therapy so that you can reach some tentative conclusion as to whether the particular individual has benefited from the approach.

Concluding remarks

This chapter has tried to illustrate some of the great challenges to tolerance faced by the people who attract autism labels. These particular challenges arise from a variety of sensitivities which cause physical and emotional distress, sensitivities of which those working with them may be unaware or which they may underestimate in terms of the degree of distress or discomfort which they cause. Day-to-day, unpredictable exposure to painful or frightening stimuli, can contribute to a lowered sense of well being. The person may start to opt out in order to avoid potentially distressing situations and this may impact upon overall quality of life. There are many ways in which help can be offered. Some are simple and relatively easy to put into place, others are more complex and resource intensive. Some are well validated, some not. However, if the problem causes distress or significantly impacts upon quality of life, then we owe it to the person to take the time and make the effort to offer the help that is needed.

CHAPTER 10

Motivation

What this chapter is about

The general concept of motivation used here refers to the conditions under which people are able to do the best that they can do and perhaps even achieve things that they have rarely been known to achieve – the idea of 'peak performance'. Much of the rest of this book is relevant to the subject of motivation. However, this chapter provides a particular focus for this general topic and also describes some specific interventions that target motivation – interventions aimed at increasing the likelihood that the person will change behaviour in the desired direction. It is about how we can help people to act competently and to inhibit inappropriate behaviours as much of the time as possible by working on the motivation to do those positive things that they sometimes, but not always, do. It is about the day-to-day fluctuations in behaviour that are not part of deeper, underlying issues to do with well being and lack of competence.

Motivation – some introductory remarks

Motivation is a messy concept. It combines aspects of the individual person, aspects of the way the environment is structured and transactions between the two. Some people are said to be more motivated than others – they will persevere on difficult tasks, tolerate discomfort more than others, work in the absence of external rewards. It is unlikely, however, that 'being motivated' is an enduring and general characteristic of a person but rather a reflection of individual history and current circumstances. In particular, motivation may reside in the tasks that people are asked to do – people are more likely to persevere with tasks that deliver meaningful outcomes for them. These outcomes may be something extrinsic, outside of and not related directly to the task, attached in an arbitrary way – for example, praise, admiration or money. Outcomes may be intrinsic – just the experience of completing the task itself is rewarding, and this may reflect sensory or intellectual characteristics of the task. Intrinsic outcomes may in turn be linked to some enduring personal characteristics (I am the kind of person who generally enjoys ... puzzles, solitude, sports). The more meaningful the pay offs and the more immediately that they occur the more motivated the person will be – in other words, he will be more likely to continue using behaviours or persisting at tasks that bring these pay offs. Persistence is therefore not so much a characteristic of the individual as a characteristic of the interface between the particular individual and the particular task. Persistence can be especially strong if the pay offs do not occur every time, but on a rather random basis that makes it hard for the person to predict exactly when the pay off will (or will not) occur. The more experience that a person has of things sometimes working out well if he sticks at them, the more 'persistent' he will be.

Motivation is therefore about how personally important outcomes are achieved through particular behaviours. The outcomes that are important to individuals reflect individual needs, wants and preferences, some momentary or transient, some longer-term. However, there is another aspect of motivation to which we will draw attention. This is a notion of motivation that passes between one person and another rather than between a person and a task. Let us take as an example what is involved in coaching. Great coaches combine two elements – an intellectual element around teaching skills, working out tactics and game plans; and a motivational element which inspires players to do the best that they can do...and more. This motivational element is almost a physical force, a transmission of energy that includes a range of specific interpersonal elements – praise and encouragement, forceful insistence and direction, the cranking up of arousal levels or the bringing of them down to get to the optimal level associated with peak performance. It is the element of passion which inspires players. It can be exuberant. It is undoubtedly urgent. But great coaches never rely on intimidation and punishment, denigration and humiliation to get the job done. There is something here about how motivation (the desire or drive to do something) can be communicated. It passes from one person to another, so that the person, hitherto unmotivated by the outcomes that a particular task has to offer, now is highly motivated to do the task. It is not just about an individual characteristic or an arrangement of rewards but it is about a relationship. This translates into some very practical motivational strategies. Whilst we can make very good use of extrinsic pay offs to influence behaviour we also believe that it is important to try to communicate more directly to people our belief in them and the importance that we attribute to their mastering new skills, keeping on trying even if things are not going well, coping with things that they find difficult and holding in check those impulses which lead to trouble.

And herein lies a puzzle that we see often in our work, a puzzle to which we have referred a number of times in this book. People who attract autism labels have a hard job reading social situations and the thoughts and feelings of others. Yet they seem to have no difficulty sensing the feelings of others around them. They sense if people dislike them, if people are frightened of them or feel hostile towards them; and this sense is expressed by increases in negative arousal in response to such social dynamics. If this impression holds true, then people with autism should also be able to pick up on positive feelings and respond to motivational coaching. And of course we all know that some individuals can get people with the label of autism to do and to tolerate things that no-one else can get them to do or tolerate. This is not just a matter of specific technique but it is also, we believe, a matter of the positive belief and inspiration that is communicated at the emotional level between the 'coach' and the person with autism.

How lack of motivation may contribute to behavioural difficulties

Leaving aside the more inspirational aspects of motivation, motivation more generally is about the desire or drive to achieve specific outcomes, to get one's needs and wants met. Motivations, needs and wants, can fluctuate moment to moment, day to day. Some may be longer term and sustained, reflecting aspects of our lives and personalities. The major motivational themes differ from one person to the next. Over time, our behaviours are shaped – we make more use of those behaviours that are more likely to achieve satisfaction of our wants and needs. We cease to use the behaviours that we have experienced to be less effective. When looking at the links between motivation and behavioural difficulties we need to consider the influences over motivation (what affects an individual's wants and needs) and the learning history, the relative effectiveness of the various behaviours available to an individual in getting wants and needs met. Some of these influences are outlined below.

Lack of well being

Positive motivation as a concept is closely linked to well being. If we feel miserable, stressed or unwell it is hard to do the best that we can to learn new skills, to socialize, to join in various activities, to tolerate discomfort, to concentrate or to work. These states strengthen other motivations and behaviours that satisfy those motivations – behaviours that are about escape from demands, access to social isolation, relief from pressure and avoidance of difficult situations. Such 'opting out' may be perceived by others to be troublesome and a number of the behaviours used to achieve these goals will be seen as problematic. The vulnerability of people with autism to loss of well being is relevant to any discussion of motivation.

Lack of inspirational relationships

When people with autism do not have around them people who inspire them – who humour, cajole, persuade or challenge them, who keep coming back despite constant rejections, who show clearly that they genuinely care about them doing well – then those individuals may see no reason to participate in activities which are not intrinsically re-warding for them. They will be less willing to learn important new skills which are of no particular interest to them or to work to change their behaviour to be more in line with the expectations of others. The lack of this type of relationship may be an accident of circumstances. It may be a result of the person's own behaviour. For example, as clinicians we know that severe self injury can engender despair amongst all those who support the person. We know that aggression towards more vulnerable people, in which the person appears to take pleasure, can create anger and dislike for the person. These feelings of anger and despair may lead carers to distance themselves from the person. However it is important to recognize the value to the person with autism of having within his support system at least one or two people who inspire him. It would not do for everyone to be like that. But neither will it do for no one to be like that.

Lack of motivation to follow social rules

In the course of development people generally learn to inhibit socially inappropriate behaviours because such behaviours upset others, draw unfavourable attention to the person, show the individual and the family up. The opinions of others matter. Understanding how others think and feel about our actions is, therefore, an important inhibitory resource. Conversely, understanding that other people think well of and feel positive about some of our actions tends to strengthen those actions and gives them greater priority. However, there are people – and many people with autism are like this – who do not readily consider the impact of their behaviours upon others and the opinions that others will form of them. Such social inhibitors are not readily available to the person. Personal needs and desires dominate. If the person wants something and has a way of getting it, he will use that way, irrespective of what others think and feel. This key lack of social understanding eliminates a motivation that is important in developing and sustaining prosocial behaviour.

The relative effectiveness of different behaviours

Given a choice between two behaviours to meet a particular need or desire, the likelihood is that we will make use of the behaviour which most reliably achieves this outcome for us. Unacceptable or challenging behaviours will be more likely to occur than socially appropriate behaviours if they achieve more reliably the outcomes important for the individual. For example, if you are engrossed in a task and the person tugs at your sleeve because she wants you to spend time with her you may respond by putting her off ('Not now, later') or even telling her off ('Can't you see I'm busy?'). However, if she punches her head or upturns the table she is likely to get your full and immediate attention. Put crudely, there's not as much pay off for the person keeping her act together as there is for her acting out, even if she has learned about social rules. Even if there is a positive pay off for acceptable behaviours it may be much more delayed than the pay off for problematic behaviours which tend to have an immediate impact. If such behaviours–pay off patterns are repeated consistently over time, the person will come to use the behaviour which is more effective. This is the process of differential reinforcement.

> *Matthew had good language skills. In class, his motivation to participate in formal learning activities was low. He would tell the teacher that he had had enough and push his work away. The teacher would nevertheless persist with the demands. Matthew would occasionally slap her when she did so. After two or three slaps she would often allow him to choose another activity. As this pattern was repeated, Matthew began to slap more frequently in class when he did not wish to continue with an activity. The frequency of his telling his teacher he had had enough diminished.*

It is vital to understand that this process of differential reinforcement operates whether or not the individual is consciously aware of it happening.

The relative efficiency of different behaviours

It is often the case that problematic behaviours have been practised many thousands of times over so that their performance is easy – practice makes perfect. By contrast some of the more acceptable behaviours – communication skills, social skills, arousal management skills – may be much less practised and much harder to initiate. We all try to achieve our goals in the least effortful way possible. Behaviours which are problematic to others may involve much less effort than their acceptable alternatives. Again, this process operates whether or not the individual is consciously aware of it.

Building positive motivation for appropriate behaviour

GENERAL PRINCIPLES

Building motivation is about addressing the general factors that facilitate the person wanting to be with people, learn new skills, participate in meaningful activities and to use socially appropriate behaviours. These are all tremendous challenges for people with autism – there is little intrinsic or immediate pay off for them rising to these challenges. Their participation is more likely if we pay attention to promoting physical and emotional well being (Chapter 6). It is also more likely if we pay attention to promoting positive relationships between the person and significant others (Chapter 5). This may include bringing into the person's life some people who have an 'inspirational' style. Finally, participation will be more likely if we pay attention to promoting achievement. As part of our long-term way of working together it is important that we set goals and celebrate and record any achievement of those goals. This is not so much a specific issue of rewarding specific behaviours but the notion of conveying to the person that she is an achieving and successful individual. Achievements are not just in terms of learning but also of accessing new experiences and relationships and what the person may have given to others. Thus the fact that a person finds it very, very hard to learn new things does not preclude us working on developing achievement motivation.

TIPS AND HINTS

(1) Think of building a long term record of achievement system for each individual – a central place for storing photographs, awards, videos that record the person's successes and can be gone over with the person.

Making planned use of non-contingent reinforcement

GENERAL PRINCIPLES

Providing non-contingent reinforcement is about ensuring that the person has positive things happen for no particular reason. The positive event is not related to the individual having shown appropriate behaviour. It is independent of that link. It can be an effective way of decreasing inappropriate behaviour but it will require planning in order for positive events to occur more frequently than they occur at present. Non-contingent reinforcement probably impacts in two ways. By providing the things that are important to the person we reduce the likelihood of him experiencing deprivation of these things and then accessing them through inappropriate behaviour. For example, if the person enjoys going outdoors and has learned that screaming and face slapping is followed by a walk outside, then by scheduling frequent access to the outdoors it becomes less likely that the individual will reach the point of needing to slap and scream.

Non-contingent reinforcement may also impact upon mood. The best gifts are often surprise gifts and if good things happen more often, this may lift mood. Given that many behavioural incidents are associated with negative mood, reducing the likelihood of such moods may reduce problematic behaviour (see also Chapter 6).

Planned use of non-contingent reinforcement can occur in two ways. One is relatively unsystematic. It involves establishing what are the major, powerful positive reinforcers for the individual, then doubling the frequency at which they occur. The second approach is more systematic. It requires assessing the function of the behaviour of concern to identify the particular reinforcer(s) maintaining it, calculating the average frequency of the behaviour in question and then scheduling access to the reinforcer to occur *more* frequently than the average interval that you have calculated.

TIPS AND HINTS

(1)   Use of non-contingent reinforcement is easier with small items or events that can be provided frequently.

(2)   Try the following exercise. List out under three headings the things in life that the person really likes, the things that he dislikes and the things he is neutral about. Work out a 'pleasure quotient' (PQ) by estimating the proportion of the person's time spent on the three categories then dividing the 'like' figure by the sum of the 'dislike' and 'neutral' figures. You can then set about increasing the person's PQ either by increasing access to positive experiences and/or by decreasing access to neutral and negative ones.

Making systematic use of contingent reinforcement

GENERAL PRINCIPLES

Contingent reinforcement means planning for the person to receive powerful, positive consequences for appropriate behaviours. This will increase the likelihood of appropriate behaviour. In so far as appropriate behaviours achieve more frequent reinforcement than negative behaviours, then the appropriate behaviours will increase and the negative behaviours decrease.

There are many ways to apply contingent reinforcement. Some of these are fairly simple and direct, others more complex and require more careful planning.

Simple direct reinforcement

This involves giving reinforcement immediately after a specific, agreed behaviour has occurred. Reinforcement may be natural (for example, the person asks appropriately and she is given what she asks for; the person signals appropriately that she has had enough and the activity finishes). Alternatively the reinforcement may come in the form of a bonus or treat (for example, praise; time with a preferred person or activity; a tasty snack). Natural reinforcers lead to the behaviour generalizing more readily but are sometimes hard to organize and they may not be powerful enough motivators.

Token systems

Token systems are those where behaviour is rewarded with symbols (points, stars, plastic tokens, money, stickers) which are later exchanged for goods and services (fruit, drinks, access to games, activities, outings). If the person earns the pre-agreed number of tokens they earn the pre-agreed reward. Token systems vary in complexity. In a simple system a small number of behaviours and a small number of rewards are included. Tokens can either be earned or lost through the system, but not both. There is a fixed rate of exchange (for example, a pre-agreed reward if 7 out of a possible 10 tokens are earned).

A complex system is one which includes many different behaviours, some of which we want to encourage (they will be rewarded by tokens), some of which we want to discourage (when they occur tokens are lost or forfeited). For example, tokens may be earned for practising new skills, helping out at home, completing work assignments and lost for hitting people and breaking things. There may be a variable rate of exchange and a range of reinforcers may be used (for example, there may be a highly favoured reward if the person earns 8/10 tokens, a less favoured one if he earns 6/10 tokens, and an even less favoured one if he earns 4/10 tokens or less).

Whatever the complexity, there are a number of key requirement for a token system to be effective:

(1) There have to be powerful reinforcers.

(2) You must have the right to control access to the reinforcers for which tokens are exchanged. They must only be accessible via the token system. Often such control is not permissible and this is not especially a matter of regret from our point of view.

(3) All the behaviours to be involved must be clearly stated so that the rules can be applied consistently.

(4) Care is needed in choosing the currency – points, stars, money, gambling chips, stickers – it can be motivating in and of itself.

(5) Where a variable rate of exchange is used, the tariff has to be set carefully so that the most desired items cost the most.

(6) The tariff–earnings relationship has to be set carefully so that the person has a very good chance of succeeding and getting the things that are important to him. As behaviour improves, standards can be raised but the system should always start by ensuring a high likelihood of success.

(7) Any cost element of the token system has to be set so that costs can be levied repeatedly – if everything is lost at one go, the system will fail.

(8) Preliminary teaching may be necessary to teach the value of the chosen token – learning the basic rules of exchange. It may also be necessary to start initially with frequent exchange so that there is only a minimal delay in actual reinforcement.

Once the idea is grasped, it becomes possible to work towards less frequent exchange (end of the day/week).

Token systems are dynamic. They need to move on – behaviours added in, new reinforcers added or eliminated, the tariff changed according to the individual's changing preferences. Saving schemes can be added so that bigger items can be earned, levels added so that people move on to less and less 'visible' systems.

If planning to use a complex token system:

○ Decide the specific behaviours that will earn tokens and specific behaviours that will lose tokens. Write out these rules.

○ Decide the times during which the system will operate.

○ Measure the average number of times the designated positive and negative behaviours currently occur during the operating period.

○ Work out the number of tokens to be earned and lost for occurrences of the specified behaviours in a way that ensures that the person will earn more than she can lose.

○ Price the reinforcers so that the most favoured items cost the most.

In addition to these general considerations there are some specific technical details which are relevant to particular applications.

Response cost systems

A simple response cost system awards automatically all the tokens needed to get the key reinforcer (if only one is being used) or most desirable items (if a range of reinforcers is used). When an incident of the designated unacceptable behaviour(s) occurs, a set number of tokens is lost immediately. The key requirements are the same as for any token system, it is just a simpler programme to administer once established. In order to establish a response cost system:

(1) Decide the specific behaviours designated as unacceptable.

(2) Decide on the operating hours of the programme (for example, 24 hours; 9 a.m.–3 p.m.).

(3) Calculate the number of tokens to be allocated by working out the average number of incidents likely over that time period and then doubling this number. This is the number of tokens to allocate at the start of the session, assuming that one token is to be lost for every occurrence of the behaviour.

(4) If using more than one reinforcer, set a variable exchange rate with the most favoured items costing the most.

Differential reinforcement of other behaviour

In this approach positive reinforcement (direct or token) is delivered for the behaviour of concern *not* having occurred for a pre-set period of time. Reinforcement may be direct (praise, a favourite treat, access to a favoured activity). Alternatively the programme can be run as a token system. To run a programme of this sort you need to:

(1) Decide the specific behaviour that you want to target.

(2) Monitor its current frequency to obtain the average frequency per minute/hour/day (as appropriate). Work out the average time between incidents based on this information. For example, if there are four incidents per hour, the average frequency between incidents is 15 minutes.

(3) Divide in half the average time interval between incidents derived in (2) above in order to increase the likelihood of the person succeeding. This will be the initial interval used for reinforcement. If the person manages this interval without the designated behaviour occurring, he is rewarded.

(4) Work out how many intervals there will be during the period over which you will run the token system (it may be all day or only during set parts of the day) to obtain the maximum number of tokens which can be earned.

(5) If an interval passes without incident, reinforcement (or a token) is given. If an incident occurs then the interval in which it occurs is 'lost' and no reward is delivered until after the next complete incident free interval.

(6) As the behaviour reduces to acceptable levels, gradually increase the length of the intervals, thus gradually fading out the reward system.

Differential reinforcement of lowered rates of behaviour

In this approach positive reinforcement is delivered if the behaviour of concern does not occur more than a predetermined number of times. Provided that the person keeps within that target, she is rewarded. If the target is exceeded, reinforcement is not given. The reinforcement may be direct. Alternatively the programme can be run as a simple token system. To run a programme of this nature you need to:

(1) Decide the specific behaviour that you want to target.

(2) Decide the time frame for the reward programme – will it be a class period, hourly, daily, weekly target. Monitor the current frequency of behaviour to work out the maximum number of incidents likely to occur during this time frame.

(3) Select as the initial target a number just under the maximum number recorded.

(4) Work out a system for visually representing the target and noting each time an incident occurs. For example, put marbles in a perspex tube (one more than the target); each time an incident occurs remove a marble. As long as there is at least one left at the end of the period, reward is given. If none are left, make no comment and reset the target for the next interval.

(5) If the behaviour is reliably on or under target (say, for 5–7 successive sessions), set a slightly lower target (a lower frequency of the behaviour).

(6) Continue in this fashion until the behaviour is within acceptable bounds.

TIPS AND HINTS

(1) Be careful about making the assumption that the person will not understand token systems. The role of conscious

understanding in behaviour change tends to be overestimated. This is especially true for token systems and differential reinforcement of other behaviour. These systems can be very helpful even with people said to have severe learning difficulties.

(2) Differential reinforcement of a lowered rate of behaviour probably requires more understanding than other types of systems. It is probably best done as part of a fun collaboration with the person around decreasing minor irritating habits.

(3) For token systems try using big numbers – hundreds and thousands rather than ones and twos (note how arcade and video games operate).

(4) All reinforcement systems must be set so that initial success is very likely.

(5) Make a lot of use of visual supports – interesting graphs and charts so that the person can see progress over time.

(6) In general the more someone can be involved in planning and developing the system the better...but not always. Sometimes this leads to increased anxiety and more behaviour. This may preclude using a reinforcement system. An alternative is to consider whether it is ethically acceptable to run a 'covert' system – use the approach but do not discuss it or make it explicit. This is an ethical more than a technical psychological issue.

(7) Be very careful about using reinforcement systems with people who are perfectionists and have not yet learned to tolerate mistakes.

(8) Be careful also about using reinforcement systems with people who need a rigid structure to their lives and cannot cope with uncertainty. They may find it hard to cope with the uncertainty of earning/not earning particular rewards. This may lead to an increase in anxiety and a worsening of the behaviour.

(9) Be careful about activating obsessions in token systems – if someone is likely to become obsessed over the numbers or filling in the blanks on the chart in a particular pattern it will disrupt the system and may indeed generate more behaviour problems. It is usually possible to find ways round these dilemmas...but not always.

Concluding remarks

This chapter has described ways in which we can directly influence the motivations of people with autism to behave in socially acceptable ways, to learn new skills, to tolerate events and stimuli or to inhibit problematic behaviour. The strategies described here supplement the strategies described elsewhere in this book. Motivation must be seen in the context of a person's quality of life, well being, relationships with others, ability to tolerate difficult stimuli or situations and the person's skills and understanding of social rules. If used in isolation, reinforcement systems are unlikely to succeed. Used as a supplement to other approaches, their influence upon behaviour can be significant.

CHAPTER 11

Responding to Behaviour – Some Additional Thoughts

What this chapter is about

Much of this book is about things to do that will either prevent destructive challenges arising in the first place or will enable people to move on from this way of managing their issues. In Chapter 3 we considered how to respond to behaviours that represent a threat to the safety of the individual or to others. Responding to such behaviours is determined by the level of risk posed by the behaviour either to the person or to others, regardless of the 'message' which such a response may give to the person (for example, that people give in, that the person gets his own way). But what about those behaviours that cause concern but are not frankly dangerous – verbal aggression, temper tantrums, spitting, screaming, even low risk aggressive behaviour? How should we respond when such behaviours occur? The chapter considers the issues involved in making this decision.

Issues to consider in responding to behavioural incidents

There may be a number of reasons for having a systematic response to incidents of problematic behaviour. Some of these reasons may be about reducing the behaviour. These include:

- Responding in a way to directly and immediately discourage the behaviour…short term (by punishing the person in some way).
- Responding in a way that decreases the likelihood of the behaviour over time by withholding whatever reinforcement is

thought to be the motivating force underlying the behaviour (for example, seeing through a demand rather than backing off; ignoring the behaviour rather than reacting to it).

○ Helping the individual to understand the consequence of his actions so that the behaviour changes…long term.

○ Showing and teaching the individual a more appropriate behaviour to use in the circumstance (see Chapter 7)…another long-term approach.

○ Supporting the individual to experience in a safe way the social consequences of her behaviour.

Other responses are more to do with ourselves and our own needs, rather than the direct needs of the individual. Thus, a planned response to behavioural incidents may be:

○ A means of building teamwork around the person and making the world more predictable for him, something which may be of general benefit even if it does not change the specific behaviour – for example, planning a consistent response to verbal abuse, as a way of empowering staff and carers (see Chapter 3).

○ A way of demonstrating to others that the behaviour is not acceptable. For example, suspending someone from school will rarely change the behaviour of the individual but it will demonstrate to all other pupils that the behaviour in question is not acceptable.

○ A way of meeting our need for justice to be seen to be done. Our sense of justice is a very important contributor to our behaviour, although it may rarely be acknowledged. Thus if one person hurts another we may want to punish that person not because it will change the behaviour but because 'it's only fair…he should not be allowed to get away with it'. This is the notion of retribution and it is about our own need for justice, which may also be seen as a gesture of support for victims.

It is important to be clear in one's own mind about the goals of having a planned response to behavioural incidents. Many are reasonable goals to aim for. However, goals associated with retribution or making an example of the person may not always be constructive even though they may make us feel better. This chapter will focus upon the issues involved in responding to behaviour in ways that may influence whether that behaviour occurs or not in the future.

Some ways in which the response to incidents may contribute to problematic behaviours occurring

Our response may reinforce the behaviour

Many behaviours that cause concern have an impact by creating changes around or within the person. These changes may be reinforcing (the person achieves a desired outcome through the behaviour, the behaviour may be satisfying). If the behaviour is repeatedly reinforced, learning takes place and the behaviour becomes functional.

- *I ask you to do something that you do not want to do, you spit at me, I go away and leave you alone.*

- *I have been busy doing something else, you would like some social input, you tip the furniture over and I come over to stop you.*

- *We are out shopping in the supermarket, you are feeling very stressed by the lighting, crowds and noise and having nothing to do, you start to scream and bite yourself and I take you out of the store.*

These are all reasonable responses but if the behaviour is repeatedly reinforced learning takes place and the behaviour becomes more functional. It becomes more likely that it will occur in the future when these situations are repeated. This process of reinforcement does not have to occur every time. In fact, most problematic behaviours which are longstanding achieve desired outcomes only occasionally and on a random basis. For example, it may be that sometimes we are firm with the person when we ask her to do something…but sometimes we are not, we give in; sometimes we ignore the person when he starts 'acting out'…but sometimes we do not, we respond directly to the behaviour. It is this situation – sometimes the reinforcement occurs, sometimes not – that produces the most persistent behaviours (which is why gambling is so addictive!). The way that we respond can, therefore, have a very direct influence upon the future likelihood of a behaviour and consolidate it as a learned behaviour. This can happen even if the original reason for the behaviour was quite different. Thus, a child may initially have banged his head because he was in great pain with an ear infection and then discovered that this behaviour had a very powerful effect on others in terms of people responding to his needs. The behaviour continues to work for him long after his ear infection has cleared up. A person may have first spat as part of an involuntary movement and then found it produced some very entertaining social responses – now she does it for fun.

It is important to point out that this learning can occur without consciousness – the individual may not be aware of the link between his behaviour and reinforcement, just as we may not be aware of the link between our own behaviour and reinforcement.

Our response may escalate arousal levels and trigger the release or persistence of behaviours

The behaviours with which this book is concerned tend to evoke negative feelings in other people – fear, anger, frustration, anxiety, despair. They are a source of stress for others. It is therefore quite natural to respond to these behaviours in a way that reflects these feelings. This can have two effects. Our actual response may be reinforcing and the behaviour strengthened. For example, the person may enjoy hearing our raised voice, he may enjoy the sense of control experienced by acting in a way which elicits a predictable reaction. Alternatively the emotionality of our response may increase the arousal level of the individual. People with autism labels may find it difficult to read in any explicit way the thoughts or feelings of others but may nevertheless be quite capable of registering the feelings of others and mirroring those feelings. Thus an intense, negative emotional response to a behaviour (anger, anxiety, feeling out of control) may directly increase the intensity of the individual's own negative feelings. Perhaps she senses that we are not in control and this triggers anxiety or increases her own sense of not being in control. The immediate result may be that her behaviour is immediately repeated, she becomes stuck in the behaviour or she crosses the threshold that leads from high arousal to the release of other problematic behaviours.

Our response may demonstrate the very behaviours that we are trying to reduce

Leaving aside any ethical issues (this is not in any way to diminish their importance), if caregivers respond to shouting by shouting back, to pinching by pinching back, to hair pulling by pulling hair in return, they are taking a psychological risk. The more often this kind of scenario is repeated, the greater the risk that the individual will take on board the idea that shouting and hitting are acceptable things to do, especially to people who are less 'powerful'. Thus the individual may stop shouting and hitting in the presence of the person who shouts at and hits them but persist with these behaviours with others who are less powerful or more vulnerable. The impact of such role modelling is not discussed enough in the autism literature. This may be because people with autism are thought not to be able to imitate (true of some, not most) or it may be thought that their difficulties in social understanding preclude them processing all kinds of social information (patently false). All practitioners know that many people with the label can imitate, sense feelings and often read very well the power dynamics of a situation (who has authority, who not). If such an individual is brought up around lack of control, intimidation and violence from authority figures, either directly experienced or witnessed towards others, then it can be expected that he will show similar behaviours himself. This is not an immediate effect but the effect of cumulative experience over time. The knowledge and learning is not conscious and explicit, but implicit – a rule or template is developed as to how relationships are to be conducted. It is a very troubling dynamic for some people with autism and it is one that deserves much closer study. It has very important implications for how carers need to conduct themselves around the individual.

Strategies for responding to decrease problematic behaviour

There are many strategies which can be used for responding to behavioural challenges. They vary in their effect upon behaviour. Some are general strategies aimed simply at providing a low key non-confrontational response, more to do with not escalating a situation than trying to effect a reduction in the behaviour. Other more specific strategies are aimed at reducing or changing the behaviour. Of these strategies some work quite quickly, others more gradually. The most appropriate response to use will depend upon a number of factors including the individual's level of understanding, our ability to stop or interrupt a behaviour, the ease with which a response can be applied consistently, the intrusiveness or dangerousness of the behaviour, and the particular motivations involved in the behaviour. The strategies are not mutually exclusive. Whichever strategy or strategies we adopt, it is important that our response is delivered in controlled way (see Chapter 3). Limits need to be set calmly and clearly, regardless of how anxious, angry or frustrated we may feel. It is important that our way of responding to incidents provides a positive role model for the person and for others (see Chapter 7).

Redirecting the person

GENERAL PRINCIPLES

Redirection involves refocusing the person from the behaviour of concern by directing their attention to another activity or behaviour. This is generally a sound strategy but may be particularly appropriate when:

(1) The person's level of understanding is poor and he is oblivious to the responses of others to his behaviour.

(2) The behaviour itself provides pleasure or reinforcement – as, for example, certain stimulatory or habitual behaviours.

(3) Direct interruption is likely to cause a severe behavioural reaction.

Redirection is not intended to reduce the behaviour over time but simply interrupt it in the present situation without affecting the person's anxiety and arousal level. Care is needed not to redirect to a highly favoured activity to which access is otherwise not available. This would risk reinforcing the behaviour.

> *Jenny screams, jumps and claps her hands continually. She appears to derive sensory enjoyment from this activity. The behaviour lessens when she is kept busy with alternative sensory activities. At times when the*

behaviour goes on for long periods and starts to intrude upon others, Jenny is redirected to one of these alternative activities.

TIPS AND HINTS

(1) The interpersonal style used in redirection needs to combine assertiveness with controlled arousal – a calm, clear redirection (come and sit with me, come and look at this).

(2) If you feel that you must comment on the behaviour, keep the comment short and clear, comment just once then redirect.

Encouraging a specific alternative response

GENERAL PRINCIPLES

Teaching alternative responses is a key strategy in long-term behaviour change. Once mastered, these alternative responses need to be encouraged in place of the behaviour of concern. The response will be one that:

(1) Achieves the same reinforcement as the problematic behaviour (see Chapter 7), but in a more appropriate manner (for example, pushing the plate away rather than throwing it on the floor; splashing water over one's hair rather than smearing saliva over it).

(2) Competes with the problematic behaviour (see Chapter 9), thereby preventing the problematic behaviour (for example, holding on to a carer's arm to keep oneself from running into the road).

(3) Controls high arousal (for example, taking oneself away from a situation when angry).

TIPS AND HINTS

(1) Get the person to practise using the alternative behaviour in role-play situations before getting her to use it in actual situations where the problematic behaviour is occurring,

particularly if her arousal levels are likely to be high at these times.

(2) Use appropriate prompting procedures (for example, a verbal or visual cue, a prompt card) to get the person to use the alternative response. Incorporate the cue when teaching the skill in question.

(3) Be sensitive to the effects of prompting the more appropriate alternative response on levels of arousal. If prompting increases arousal levels then be prepared to back off and redirect.

(4) Immediately reinforce use of the appropriate alternative behaviour (for example, with access to a desired activity, verbal praise).

Directly interrupting the behaviour

GENERAL PRINCIPLES

Interruption seeks to stop the behaviour quickly and directly by placing a firm boundary upon it. The responses has four elements:

(1) Defining the exact behaviour and the point at which the behaviour is to be interrupted.

(2) Gaining the person's attention.

(3) Stopping the behaviour (for example, by taking objects away, blocking hands).

(4) Redirecting the person.

Such an approach may be appropriate in situations where:

(1) The person has some social awareness so that interruption acts to 'remind' the person that she is doing something inappropriate.

(2) The behaviour is interruptible without involving significant restraint.

(3) Interruption does not trigger distress and an escalation of behaviour.

(4)   The behaviour involves a series of stages, accompanied by increasing arousal. Interruption occurs early in the sequence and is intended to halt further escalation of arousal.

When interrupting a behaviour it is important to avoid, if possible, use of the words 'no', 'don't' or 'stop'. Setting ourselves this informal rule forces us to think of what else to say and makes it easier to develop a positive statement about what we actually want to happen. Positive statements such 'Hands down' rather than 'No scratching': 'Sit down' rather than 'Stop pushing': 'Stand still' rather than 'Don't push' are more likely to get through than a negative statement because they immediately make clear what is expected. There are other reasons, too, for avoiding use of these negative words as an interruption response. One reason is that people with autism can be very literal in their interpretations of the things that we say. They may respond to the instruction 'Stop' by literally freezing in their tracks (fingers still firmly entwined in your hair!). Finally, the words 'stop' or 'don't' may be associated with negative experiences and negative behaviours and cause distress which may immediately escalate a situation.

> *Jeremy, a middle-aged man, was a gentle person for the most part, but with a history of aggressive behaviour. A support worker, whilst out with him one day, said 'Stop' quite loudly as they approached a pedestrian crossing – she had noticed that the lights had started to change. Jeremy became immediately aggressive towards her. Later he explained that he thought that when she had said 'Stop' she was telling him off and he did not understand what he had done wrong.*

TIPS AND HINTS

(1)   Develop a consistent response for gaining the individual's attention. For example, say her name first (so that the person knows the message is intended for her) then give an instruction directed at focusing the person's attention (for example, 'Look at me' or 'Hands down').

(2)   For some individuals a visual cue (for example, a red and yellow card as used for fouls in soccer; a red stop sign adapted from road signs) may help to enhance a verbal

interruption message or it may be used in place of the verbal message.

(3) Some agencies find it useful to use a single interruption response for everyone who uses their service (for example, 'Stand still, hands down').

Withholding reinforcement for the behaviour

GENERAL PRINCIPLES

This response is intended to effect a fairly rapid reduction in the behaviour. It requires being quite clear about what is the reinforcer for the behaviour (getting out of a situation, opting out of a task, sensory stimulation or pleasure, social input) and then being able to withhold the reinforcer when the behaviour occurs.

If the behaviour is reinforced by attention from others, then ignoring the behaviour and withholding social attention would be an appropriate response.

> Aisha would run up to people and clap her hands hard in front of their face. It was felt that this behaviour was reinforced by the direct reaction this usually got from others. The strategy adopted was to make no response to the behaviour (no comment, no flinching), simply carrying on with whatever the person was doing at the time.

If the behaviour is reinforced by opting out of activities or social situations, then withholding reinforcement may mean continuing to give attention (for example, persisting with a request) rather than ignoring the person.

> Mark pinched others, especially when they tried to engage him in classroom tasks. It was felt that this behaviour was reinforced by people usually moving away. The strategy adopted was to protect the arms by always wearing long sleeved clothing when working with Mark and to persist with the request until he had completed at least some of the task, before moving away.

If the behaviour is being reinforced by sensory stimulation, then withholding reinforcement would mean removing any sensory outcome which the behaviour may produce.

> *Gemma spat a lot. She would spit on the floor, then rub the saliva into the floor with her foot, gazing at it for several seconds afterwards. The visual stimulation this produced was felt to be reinforcing her behaviour. The strategy adopted was to wipe away the saliva as soon as she spat.*

Responding in a way that avoids reinforcing the behaviour is a way of effecting a steady reduction in the behaviour. It depends for its success upon correctly identifying the reinforcement that is maintaining the behaviour and withholding reinforcement with complete (100%) consistency. It is important to note that if these criteria are met (the reinforcer for the behaviour has been correctly identified and consistently withheld) then there will inevitably be an initial increase in the frequency or severity of the behaviour. This is one instance when an increase in the behaviour should be taken as a good sign and cause for celebration! As long as you keep your nerve and continue withholding the reinforcer, a reduction should begin after a few weeks and continue steadily after that. If the behaviour increases and does not start to decrease again after a few weeks, then it may be that your response is actually reinforcing the behaviour or that the intervention is not being delivered consistently.

TIPS AND HINTS

(1) Before deciding that you are going to withhold reinforcement for a behaviour, ask yourself the following questions:

- Given that we know that the behaviour will get worse initially, how bad is it likely to get?

- Can we still withhold reinforcement for the behaviour if it gets as bad as we anticipate?

- Can everyone involved within the environment where we plan to use this strategy withhold and continue to withhold reinforcement?

If the answer to any of these questions is 'No' then withholding reinforcement should not be adopted as a strategy. If it is, the long-term result might be that the person learns (consciously or unconsciously) that persistence pays and this will make the behaviour harder to change in the future. Worse, more extreme behaviours may be shaped as we give in to these, thereby allowing reinforcement to occur.

(2) Ignoring a person (or turning your back on them) is not the same as ignoring a behaviour. This is a direct action which gives the person clear feedback that you are responding to the behaviour. If you are going to ignore, it means just that – acting as though the behaviour is not occurring and carrying on as you had been intending to do.

(3) If you feel that some response is unavoidable try to do it in a way that does not allow the behaviour to redefine the situation. Thus, if you were going to do some reading with the other students, deal with the behaviour and get back to the reading; if you had planned to shop at the supermarket, deal with the behaviour but get back to doing at least a small amount of shopping; if you had planned to watch your favourite TV show, deal with the behaviour but get back to watching at least some of the show. When a behavioural incident redefines altogether what you had intended to happen, that is when the behaviour is most likely to be reinforced and strengthened. In addition, keep the social response as undemonstrative as possible – minimum speech, minimum eye and physical contact, a firm assertive redirection. Control your arousal level.

(4) Always remain focused upon what you want the person to do now – avoid discussing the behaviour and telling the person what you do *not* want them to do. Keep the focus on what it is you actually want to happen now.

(5) Avoid any reinforcement as soon as the behaviour stops. Do *not* reinforce cessation of behaviour. Wait for a period of time when no instances of inappropriate behaviour have occurred

or wait until the person does something which is positive and reinforce that but do not reinforce immediately after the behaviour has stopped.

Imposing a cost upon behaviour

GENERAL PRINCIPLES

Behaviour can clearly be changed by punishment. Punishment in this sense occurs when an event follows immediately and every time after an incident and there is a decrease in the frequency of the behaviour (this is to be distinguished from retribution where there is no implication that the behaviour itself will necessarily change). Individuals vary in the events that will act as punishers. What is a punisher for one may be a reinforcer for another. Thus, keeping a person back from a group outing to a café following an incident may be an unwanted consequence for the person who enjoys outings and food, a reinforcing event for the person who dislikes being part of a group and likes the peace and quiet of an empty house. Withdrawing attention from a person following an aggressive act may be an unwanted consequence for the person who likes attention, but reinforcing for the person who enjoys his own company and dislikes others talking to him.

Punishment clearly forms part of everyday parenting. It is also a part of society's way of controlling the behaviour of its citizens. From the point of view of this book, however, there are a number of problems.

○ Punishment does not enhance the individual's resources and coping capacities and we believe strongly that behaviour change must be centred upon building these areas of functioning.

○ In the field of developmental disabilities professional carers have in the past relied heavily upon punishment to change behaviour, using some extraordinary and arbitrary means to do so (examples include slapping, pinching, squirting lemon juice in the mouth, pain shock, breaking ammonia capsules, squirting water into the face). Such approaches not only form part of a repeated historical pattern of professional care degenerating into frank abuse, but have also contributed to the burden of stigma that people with disabilities have to bear in our society. They have contributed to the perception that people with disabilities should be treated differently from the ways that we treat other human beings, that things that we would find intolerable if done to ourselves are legitimate to do to people with disability labels.

○ Advances in knowledge in recent years have provided many new insights and positive approaches to work on behavioural and emotional issues.

We therefore rule out in this book any use of arbitrary and aversive interventions. We do not, however, rule out the use of costs which can be used as a form of punishment, but which do not involve the use of arbitrary events. These are what we might call response costs. We use strict criteria for the acceptability of cost interventions.

(1) Costs used should be the kinds of costs used effectively to change the behaviour of other people – people without disabilities. They must be acceptable to all those directly involved (never stigmatizing or degrading or frightening). Anyone who is going to implement the cost must agree with the statement 'If I had a behaviour in need of change, I would accept this kind of cost when I acted in this way'.

(2) Costs must be relevant to the behaviour. They must be in some way a natural consequence for the behaviour so that the person learns the natural social consequences of behaving in ways considered unacceptable. Thus, if money is important to the person and he steals or break things that belong to others, it may be appropriate that he at least contribute to the replacement cost of the item. If trips to the supermarket are important to the person and she is abusive and disruptive just prior to the trip, then it may be appropriate to keep her back from the trip, so that she can learn that others do not want to be in her company when she acts in this way. If a person enjoys being around people and is aggressive to others in the room, then it may be appropriate to ask him to leave and spend time on his own, so that he learns that others will not tolerate such behaviour in their company.

(3) Costs should be as brief and small as possible – just long enough for the message to be effective (this will vary between individuals) and until any ongoing behaviour stops. Thus, if paying a small contribution to the replacement of broken items is effective, then it may not be necessary to ask the person to pay the whole cost of replacement; if being kept back from one trip to the supermarket provides an effective message, then it is not justifiable to ban the person from trips to the supermarket for the remainder of the month; if asking the person to leave the room results in rapid cessation of disruption, then it is appropriate to allow the person back as soon as the behaviour is appropriate rather than insist the person does not return for the rest of the evening.

(4) Costs must be agreed in advance, part of a plan – not levied on an impulse and without control on the size of the cost.

(5) Costs should always be used in the context of an assessment of the individual's needs and in conjunction with a range of positive and constructive approaches to meet those needs – approaches aimed at preventing behaviour and providing the individual with skills and coping resources to help prevent behaviour in the long term.

In addition to these criteria of acceptability, costs need to meet certain technical standards if they are to be used effectively:

(1) The behaviour on which the cost is to be levied must be very clearly defined.

(2) It must be possible to levy the cost very quickly after the behaviour has occurred, so that the person associates the cost with the behaviour in question.

(3) It must be possible to levy the cost every time the behaviour occurs.

(4) There must be demonstrable evidence over time that the cost intervention does in fact reduce the behaviour. It is not always easy to predict in advance whether a cost intervention will work, whether the cost is meaningful to the person. However,

it should become clear within a reasonably short space of time whether the cost is having any impact on the behaviour. There is no justification for maintaining a cost intervention without evidence of fairly rapid change.

Where it is felt to be impossible to meet criteria (2) and (3) it may be appropriate to consider levying costs via a token system (see Chapter 10).

Under the conditions discussed above, cost-based interventions may have a role to play in helping the individual develop the resources to inhibit problematic behaviours.

TIPS AND HINTS

(1) Rules about the individual's behaviour should be set in advance and the person involved as much as possible in setting the rules.

(2) Rules usually work better if presented as universal rules (what we all must do) rather than personal ones (what you must do).

(3) Rules should be displayed in ways the person will understand (using line drawings, cartoons, writing). Alongside information about negative behaviour (the behaviours that the person should not show) and the cost that will be levied upon these behaviours there should be information about positive behaviours which are expected (appropriate ways that the person should behave).

(4) The rules should be referred to regularly, not just when incidents occur.

(5) Decide whether warnings are given before a cost is levied, so that the person has a 'chance' to stop the behaviour. This decision should be based upon knowledge of the individual. If warnings are to be given, however, be very clear about how many. Be consistent.

(6) Once the rule is established and the cost system is agreed, do not get drawn into discussions about them at the moment the rule is broken and you are imposing the cost. Do not get

involved in debates about 'fairness'. Respond simply with 'It's the rule'.

(7) Make sure that the cost is imposed in a calm but firm manner, without any personal criticism of the individual.

(8) As soon as the cost has been levied and the behaviour stopped a positive attitude should be immediately adopted towards the individual.

Developing understanding through explanations

GENERAL PRINCIPLES

Providing rules in advance gives the person clear information about what is expected in given circumstances – what behaviours are appropriate, what behaviours are not acceptable. Levying costs for inappropriate behaviours may act as a direct disincentive for violating the rules. Providing explanations may enable the person to gain insight and understanding about the reason for the cost and the importance of the rules. Such insight may over the longer term develop into a key inhibitory resource for the individual. This 'cognitive' approach can be combined with the more direct behavioural strategies (withholding reinforcement, levying costs). Explanations can be given in many ways and at varying levels of complexity, depending upon the individual's level of understanding.

TIPS AND HINTS

(1) An explanation can be given after the incident – once the incident is over and the situation calmed – about the effect of the behaviour in question. The explanation needs to be concrete and to make specific links (pinching hurts, kicking makes people cry). Such an explanation needs to be brief. The language needs to be carefully chosen and if possible should use words commonly used by the individual (if the person refers to being agitated as 'having a crisis' then we should mention that we, too, have a 'crisis' when the person's behaviour disrupts other people's access to pleasurable activities).

(2) Rules and explanations can be presented as a short written story or fact sheet, using the format described by Carol Gray (1994b) for writing social stories (see Chapter 7) to supplement other information. Such stories or fact sheets provide reassurance about the feelings that the person may be having (anger, frustration) plus information about appropriate coping strategies to use and the positive effects of using appropriate coping strategies for the person and for others.

Delroy would frequently become very agitated and then start to lash out at those around him and throw things around the room. A short personalized 'story' was written for him to supplement other interventions. 'Getting angry about things is natural. Everyone gets angry sometimes. There are good ways to help myself when I get angry. I can count slowly to 10. I can go and listen to some classical music or I can write in my diary. It is important to make good choices when I get angry as this will keep me and others safe. When I make good choices it helps me to calm quicker, it makes my teachers proud of me and it makes the other children happy because they are not disturbed and can carry on with what they are doing. I will try to remember to make good choices when I get angry.'

(3) If using stories or fact sheets to supplement rules, read these regularly to the person. Have others read them to the person. Do not make behavioural incidents the trigger for reading them.

(4) If you want the person to start thinking more about his own behaviour and trying to understand it, set time aside regularly to do this (see also Chapter 3). Do not make incidents the triggers for such sessions – it is not the best time for analytic thinking and it runs the risk of either reinforcing the behaviour, escalating arousal or causing the individual to fixate on the behaviour. Rather, pick a regular time – daily, weekly as appropriate. Structure the sessions so that they follow a predictable pattern.

(5) Try supporting verbal discussions about problematic situations which have occurred for the person with a visual representation of the event using, for example, the comic strip conversations format described in Chapter 7.

Concluding remarks

Responding to problematic behaviour cannot be avoided. When we respond inconsistently and with high emotionality, we are helping neither the person nor the situation. A carefully planned response, consistently applied, is always to be preferred. There are a number of outcomes that we may seek to achieve by such a planned response and we have tried to identify those, so that the rationale for the plan can be clear. Just as there are a number of possible outcomes, so too there are a range of strategies and combinations of strategies for achieving the outcomes desired and these can be pursued individually or in combination.

Recent years have provided us with many new insights and approaches to work on behavioural and emotional issues for people with autism labels. It is vital that whatever strategy is used to respond to non-dangerous behavioural incidents, it is done in combination with a whole range of positive approaches. These approaches are aimed at avoiding the need for the person to show the behaviour in the first place and at equipping the person with the skills and coping resources for managing more effectively day-to-day stresses. Responding to incidents is the last thing to consider and it is no coincidence that this chapter comes at the end, not at the start, of the book's main section, detailing constructive approaches to supporting people with autism around their behavioural issues.

Part III

Making it Happen

There is often said to be a gap between knowledge and practice. Well-validated supports may not be implemented routinely. This section looks at some of the issues that can help to bridge that gap – that raise the likelihood that people whose behaviour causes concern receive in a sustained way constructive supports to move on in their lives.

CHAPTER 12

Expectations

What this chapter is about

This chapter looks at the question of expectations. It will seek to strike a balance. We feel very positive about people's capacities for moving on in their lives and about the ability of others to promote and encourage those capacities. However, we are aware that moving on will not always mean complete and total elimination of behaviour (we will look at some of the reasons for this). If our expectation is that our work should lead to complete and enduring elimination of behaviours that concern us, then we will sometimes be disappointed and may feel that we have failed; worse, that the person in question is unchangeable and unpredictable. We may abandon doing helpful things just because we have not 'solved' the problem. We will therefore be looking at ways to ensure that our expectations are positive but realistic, to make sure that we celebrate changes small and large and that we communicate this sense of achievement to the person(s) that we are supporting.

Human behaviour changes...but fluctuates

It may be helpful to stop thinking about behaviour in isolation and to think more in terms of people as people, as whole systems with different modes of functioning. A person may be in challenging mode, playful mode, childish mode, adult mode, determined mode, despairing mode. Such modes involve a number of systems – behavioural, emotional (feelings), physical (health), cognitive (attitudes, beliefs and interpretations). Behavioural work can then be redescribed as supporting people to experience these various and changing modes without doing so in ways that are dangerous or harmful to themselves and to others. Most people can already do this some of the time. Our task is to find ways of extending this time. In some ways this is like juggling – we want the balls to stay in the air. This will require a complex arrangement which includes the skill of the juggler, concentration of the juggler, stamina of the juggler, emotional state of the juggler, level of distraction in the environment, wind speed, temperature, light, dynamic properties of the ball. A change in one or more of these variables may send the balls crashing to the earth, a careful arrangement may keep the balls in the air for a very long period of time. So too it seems to us when considering the ball that we call human behaviour.

Exercise 12.1

About Behaviour Change

(1)   List out the behaviours that you have engaged in during your life that other people would regard as problematic, challenging, or of concern.

(2)   Cross out those that you have stopped doing altogether (they never now occur). How many of those are there?

(3)   Take one at a time those that still continue. For each behaviour selected, identify the factors that determine whether the behaviour occurs or not, whether it occurs more or less frequently, more or less intensely.

(4)   Take one at a time those that you have stopped altogether. For each one list out the factors that have enabled you to move on from engaging in the behaviour and that prevent you from going back to behaving in this way.

We hope that Exercise 12.1 illustrates some important things about behaviour. One is that many behaviours remain part of our repertoire long term – sometimes they are always there but vary as to the extent of their presence, sometimes we stop showing behaviours for a time but they do come back under certain circumstances. We are not cured of our behaviours, nor do we unlearn them. This also serves to remind us of the second important point, that our behaviour is lawful, that it is subject to predictable influences. The comings and goings do not represent random fluctuations, are not unpredictable (though others may fail to understand the reasons) but rather reflect adaptations to the world around us and the world within us (see Chapter 2). Contrast this with the extensive attachment of the word unpredictable to the behaviour of people who attract autism labels.

There is a third thing that the exercise may have illustrated. That is that we have been able to leave behind certain behaviours in so far as we have been able to develop over time some key protective resources.

Longer-term change requires the development of certain key resources

We have already acknowledged that all humans engage in behaviours that other humans find challenging or problematic. Yet most of us are not identified publicly as a person with challenging or problematic behaviour. People are not keeping records of our behaviour, having case conferences, designing and implementing formal intervention plans. The people with whom this book is concerned are, however, identified publicly as showing problematic behaviour that justifies formal intervention. What is the difference here? Part of the answer is that we have core resources that enable us to function in socially acceptable ways, that enable us to cope with the day-to-day hassles and stresses in ways considered acceptable and that facilitate some forgiveness when we act out our problems. These resources include

- Knowledge – knowing about the consequences of our actions, and about how others will think about us, understanding the ideas of justice and fair play.

- Skills – being able to communicate to people about our needs and to persuade them to make some accommodation for us.

- ○ Social support – having a network of relationships that provide us with social-emotional support, encouragement and practical help, experiences of intimacy, affirmation of worth and models of socially competent behaviour…and who don't tell on us every time we step out of line!

- ○ A lifestyle that works well enough for us – we function better socially in so far as we are living in the places, doing the kinds of work and leisure activities, having the sorts of social relationships that work for us. If there is a reasonable fit between us and the life that we lead then we function better socially.

What this is turn illustrates in painful and graphic detail is why people with autism labels may find it so hard to sustain good enough social functioning. It indicates that building some of the key resources (skills and knowledge) upon which we all rely is a long-term business. Whilst there are ways in which behaviour can be changed in the short term (and very useful ways at that) the key issues that we are dealing with are long term. It also illustrates that some of the key resources lie outside of the individual – they lie in the social support system and style of life within which the person is embedded. Addressing these latter factors need not always be a long-term matter but it may certainly mean challenging the way that society provides services for people with disabilities. The lives that people without disabilities think are good for people with disabilities will not necessarily coincide with the life that would work for the particular individual(s) with whom the readers of this book are concerned.

Thus, whilst there are ways in which behaviour can be changed in the short term, many of the key issues that we are dealing with are long term. These issues can be addressed but they take time and therefore it is only to be expected that any change in the short term may be relatively fragile until some of the longer-term issues are addressed. To call something long term is not, however, to imply large scale, dramatic, 'curative' interventions.

Making changes – what really counts

Behaviour change takes time

There appears to be a widely held notion that behaviour problems are like illnesses and that what we are looking for is a cure. Certainly it would be nice if there were things that we could do that would be guaranteed to produce large, long-lasting behavioural change quickly and with minimal effort. That is why the use of drugs is so popular despite the very limited evidence of their usefulness. It is true that some behaviour programmes or environmental alterations can produce rapid (matter of weeks) change. Some drugs may also have a similarly speedy impact. However, by and large human behaviour change of all kinds takes time and is usually marked by fluctuations. We do not readily leave behind old habits and old ways and the behaviours with which this book is concerned are nothing if not well established.

Behaviour change is not spectacular

Human behaviour change is by and large an unspectacular business. Dramatic cures, overnight transformations are the stuff of myths and legends. Real and secure change comes from the accumulation of little (and not so little) things done persistently and consistently.

Behaviour change takes place in the real world of the person

Real change comes when effective things occur as part and parcel of everyday life. The idea that change occurs by removing people to special places for treatment and training is also the stuff of myths and legends. Real change takes place in the real world and is effected by the real people who operate in that world – the people said to have disabilities and those who live and work with them on a day-to-day basis. There is a role for outside experts in the same way that sports teams have a role for coaches and physiotherapists; but at the end of the day it is the players on the field who do the business.

Hence this book has focused upon practical things that can be woven into everyday life which, we believe, more truly represents what is known about significant human behaviour change. Even in the most extreme of circumstances, we can all play a constructive role and whilst there are things that we all need to learn, there are things that we all can do to help. Change will not come easy. It will require great perseverance but it will come.

Effecting change

It takes a team

One of the underlying themes of this book is that good understanding and ideas come when those who know a person put their heads together to solve a problem jointly and work together on implementing the ideas generated. Given the stressful nature of the behaviours with which we are concerned and the sometimes erratic course of progress, a group is often able to provide support and encouragement to its members. The quality of such a team approach can be enhanced if the team is joined by people who have specialist knowledge and expertise relevant to the problem in hand. Working through serious behavioural issues is not something to be done alone and unsupported – it is something to be done together with other people who share the concern and are willing to join the effort. Better results can be expected under these circumstances.

This is the notion of a core group that includes the person with identified disabilities, kith and kin, friends and those paid to provide support. Such a group may seek expert consultation with people who have something to offer but do not join the team. The team retains ownership of the work that will be done and is in the position to make decisions about this.

This is a very big topic that we can only touch upon here. However, the point to stress is that we can have higher expectations for progress where the members of a group are working together to support the person than where an individual is battling through unsupported or, worst of all, where the potential core group members are actually working against each other.

Keeping in touch with current research and the growth of knowledge

One of the reasons that a core group may seek external consultation is to make sure that it is accessing the latest findings coming in from research work. The field of autism has been an explosive one in terms of the growth of knowledge. It receives a relatively high and sustained research investment compared to other developmental disabilities and that investment has been very fruitful. Much progress has been made in understanding better the needs of people with autism but there is so much still to learn. We are at the beginning of the learning curve not near the end.

Thus our expectations of progress will always be relative to the current state of knowledge. We can do more now than we could 25 years ago and our expectations are much higher. Yet there remain many times when we struggle to make sense of what is going on and struggle to make significant progress. Sometimes that will be because we have not used all the knowledge available, sometimes it will be because there is not enough knowledge. The struggle to understand goes on and the reader can be sure that a book like this in another 25 years time will have a lot more to offer than this one.

Concluding remarks

Behaviour change requires thoughtful and sustained effort by the person and those who support her. Change may take time and the course of progress may be fluctuating. Some of the important work is very long term. It is therefore important that behavioural work is considered more as a marathon than as a sprint – anyone can do it but it takes great perseverance and a lot of support.

CHAPTER 13

Implementation

What this chapter is about

It is one thing to understand a problem or to have some good ideas about how to solve it. It is another to turn these thoughts into sustained action plans. This is especially important in view of the points made in the last chapter about the need for persistent and consistent work on an everyday basis. This chapter will look at the processes and arrangements that make it more likely that good ideas will turn into sustained practice.

The discussion will be organized around a series of steps. These steps are what one might call 'notional' – they refer to activities that need to occur but do not prescribe how they should occur. So for example there is no implication that every step requires a meeting or that every step has to be written up in a document. These kinds of decisions will depend upon local circumstances and contexts. Consideration will need to be given as to how to adapt the ideas here to the communities and service organizations of the reader.

Formalizing structures and processes

(1) Identify the stakeholders

Once a person's behaviour has been identified as a cause for concern and requiring some planned action, the first step is to identify those who have a keen interest in working on this problem and have them all communicating with each other.

(2) Identify a process manager

Once the preliminary group of stakeholders has begun communicating an early decision needs to be made as to who is going to see to it that the various steps are completed, that assessments are carried out, plans made and implemented, results monitored. It matters less who takes the job on than that the job is allocated. It may be a parent, teacher, therapist, psychologist, social worker, the person whose behaviour is of concern, whoever is willing. The role of the individual needs to be acknowledged by all stakeholders.

(3) Clarify core group and consultants

It may be that the initial group needs to add some 'permanent' members who will join in the whole process of working through the problems. It may also help to identify if there are 'consultants' upon whom the group can call in a more limited way. A consultant may have specialist knowledge in relevant areas and would agree to be available to the core group for advice and support but would not be a full time group member, working through every stage.

(4) Clarify communication channels

The process manager needs to work out with the group and consultants how information will be collected, decisions made and reviewed. It may involve regular meetings but there are plenty of other ways of working together – contacts by telephone, fax or e-mail, video conferencing, writing notes to each other. Provided that someone is managing the process, the option or combination of options can be chosen that are best suited to local conditions.

(5) Identify a specific focus for the work of the group

There may be many concerns about the behaviour of an individual. Group members may refer to problems in rather generic ways that can easily mean different things to different people (tantrums, outbursts, aggression). It is important to follow two golden rules:

- Be very specific when describing the behaviours that you are going to focus on
- Limit your discussions to one behaviour at a time.

It will be important to list out all the specific behaviours that are of concern to group members and then for the group to decide which specific behaviour(s) it is going to focus work on. Always err on the side of working on very specific issues rather than trying to solve all concerns at one go. When you solve one problem you may find that you have automatically solved another…but you may not. If you start by trying to work on several things at once the risk of confusion and inconsistency rises dramatically.

(6) Establish a behaviour monitoring system

Once a specific behaviour has been identified as the focus of concern it is important to establish a system for monitoring that behaviour. This will be an essential element in judging whether or not progress is being made. Whilst there are some technical considerations in behaviour monitoring that are beyond the scope of this book, the basis is simple. There needs to be some measure of the frequency or duration of behaviour that is taken regularly. This may, for example, be an incident-recording sheet with a tick mark for each incident. These totals need to be added on a daily, weekly or monthly basis and this figure entered on a graph. The graph will enable the group to tell at a glance whether the behaviour is reducing – whether it is occurring less often this week compared to last week to a month ago to six months ago to a year ago and so on and so on. This is the only sure way to tell if the interventions are helping. Our memory is simply not adequate for this job. Keeping such records need not be time consuming but they must be kept and someone must have the responsibility for keeping the graph up to date. This is such a powerful aid to decision making that it is alarming how often it is absent in practice.

(7) Identify and carry out some assessment work on the focus behaviour

The work here is not so much to count the behaviour but to identify why it may be occurring, what are the factors that contribute to this behaviour happening and continuing to happen. Assessment is an important topic in its own right and is not fully covered in this book. It is likely to involve observing the behaviour and keeping records when incidents occur, identifying situations and circumstances when the behaviour is very unlikely to occur, interviewing the person with autism if possible and interviewing those who know the person well. Specialist assessments from a communication therapist, an occupational therapist, a psychologist and a psychiatrist may be sought at this stage, to see if there are additional relevant perspectives on the behaviour in question.

(8) Summarize the assessment work into a story (formulation) of why the behaviour occurs

There is no point in gathering information unless it is summarized and interpreted. The observations, interviews, checklists and specialist assessments need to be brought together to extract the factors that may be contributing to the focus behaviour. There will almost always be more than one contributor and we will not always feel that we have identified all the contributors. But summarizing what seems likely to be contributing to the behaviour occurring is a vital step to take before getting on to 'what do we do?' At this stage the story that we tell is just a theory which seems plausible in light of the evidence gathered. It is neither true nor false. Whether it is helpful or not will be determined when we take action. If we follow through on the implications of our story and the behaviour gets less then it looks as if we are on the right track. If we follow through and the behaviour does not reduce then it does not mean that the story was wrong – we may need to do more things or do them for longer. However, it will alert us to the possibility that we may be on the wrong track and that we may need to carry out more assessment work. It is important to develop in the core team these ideas of detection work, possibilities, theories that at the end of the day stand or fall on the results that they achieve for the individual. This gets away from the arguments about who is right and who is wrong – who has the 'best' insights. Arguments about who has the right answer often split a team and encourage inconsistency and fragmentation of effort. Working on the notion of building a shared view, learning from the behaviour of the person and being prepared to adjust our opinions in the light of information incoming from the person, keeps the individual with autism at the centre of the group's attention and cuts into any personal issues which team members may have.

(9) Identify all relevant interventions that follow from the 'story'

Once the assessment work is summarized into a working theory the next step is to list out all the interventions that would be relevant if that story was true – if this is what I think is going on, what would be the logical things to do in order to enable the person to behave in this way less often?

(10) Prioritize the interventions

In all situations resources are likely to be limited. It is unlikely that it will be possible to do all the things that might be relevant. Interventions identified as important will need to be categorized into:

- ○ Those that the group definitely feels willing and able to do

- ○ Those that the group sees as relevant but are not going to be done either because the group does not feel competent to do them or because they do not have the time or energy to do them.

From the list of those that the group feels willing and able to do, the next stage is to identify those that the group is definitely going to do. The remaining interventions are then divided into three groups:

- ○ Those that may be done later

- ○ Those for whom additional resources will be sought

- ○ Those about which nothing is going to be done at this stage.

(11) Identify who needs to do what by when to make the prioritized interventions happen

It needs to be made clear how a good idea is going to be turned into actual practice. This means allocating responsibilities and setting time targets.

(12) Identify who needs to do what by when to seek additional resources

It is necessary to clarify responsibilities for seeking the additional resources needed to carry out some of the other interventions identified as relevant in 10.

(13) Clarify the review mechanisms

Make sure that the group is clear about when and how the interventions will be reviewed, when and how the group will review the actions taken to secure more resources. At this point make sure that the necessary documentation is in order.

(14) Implement, monitor, review

It is only at this point that the planned interventions get going. Through the planned review mechanisms the group learns whether the person is being supported effectively. If the behaviour is getting less, make sure that fact is celebrated – it is a great compliment to the person and the support team. If there is no change, then there are a number of options for the group to consider:

- Do nothing, just continue...maybe the interventions need longer before they have an impact

- Add an intervention from the list of ideas identified as relevant

- Drop an intervention

- Take a step back and carry out some more assessment work.

It is hard to give more specific guidelines about how these decisions should be made. However as a rule of thumb any intervention identified as relevant should be given at least a month's trial (unless it is demonstrably having very adverse effects, is on all objective measures making matters much worse).

Concluding remarks

It is very clearly the case that what is known to be good practice is hard to get implemented and sustained. Good ideas may not get implemented at all, may get implemented half-heartedly, may get implemented and abandoned quickly. On the other hand interventions of no demonstrable benefit may be sustained. Helpful interventions are sometimes fun but they may be difficult, boring or aversive for the people charged with carrying them out. Immediate results will not always be apparent. That is why it is essential to construct a work system that will help keep the behaviour of supporters on the tracks that are effective for the people that they are supporting. The natural consequences of doing helpful things cannot be relied upon to sustain people doing those things.

CHAPTER 14

Service Provision Issues

What this chapter is about

This chapter is about the characteristics of services that are more likely to do a good job of providing positive and sustained support to people with autism whose behaviour causes serious concern. People whose behaviour causes grave concern have a habit of being excluded from services, being confined in ever more restrictive settings and of being abused by those paid to support them. It is hard to find good quality behaviourally-competent services. It is also hard to define what constitutes a good quality service. This is what the chapter tries to do – to specify the conditions under which a service is likely to operate in ways and deliver outcomes that we call 'good quality'. This of course begs the question as to what we mean by 'good quality'. We define this as a service that enables the following outcomes to be achieved…as a result of service activity the individual:

- Finds a way of life that works for him/her
- Achieves the maximum possible sense of physical and emotional well being
- Behaves less often in ways that are generally regarded as socially unacceptable and that raise the likelihood of social exclusion.

Introductory remarks

The chapter is written primarily in terms of an 'outsider' looking at a service and having to judge whether the service is likely to be competent – thus it is written primarily to inform consumers (people with autism and their families), purchasers or inspectors. However the aspects of service provision discussed here would be relevant to service managers who need also to answer the question – how do I know if my service is doing/going to do a good job supporting someone whose behaviour is challenging?

The chapter will attempt to answer this question in terms of general characteristics that apply whether the service is for children or adults, educational, employment, leisure or home provision, 'special' or 'mainstream'. All services that support effectively the people with whom this book is concerned will need to be competent in the areas identified.

Of course they will need to be competent in other areas too – the present list is not a complete specification of the ideal service, it focuses upon the competencies relevant to good quality, positive behavioural support. Even within this more restricted area it is perhaps unrealistic to expect that services will function well in every single area identified. Nevertheless a service should be functioning well in most of them and be working on achieving competence in the others if it is to be able to deliver high-quality support.

The ideas that follow come mainly from experience rather than from any formal theories or research. The organization of the chapter will be in terms of a series of broad statements about key service characteristics. For each of these characteristics there will be a general outline of what is meant by the statement and specific things that can be observed (evidence of competence) if a service is functioning well in the area under consideration. The order of the statements does not reflect any particular priority.

Characteristics of good quality behavioural services
(1) A general philosophy that is respectful and inclusive
The service should see itself as providing for people who vary widely in their functioning and be trying to find ways to accommodate and include individual differences. It should celebrate diversity and emphasize respect for the individual. A rigid and inflexible service that sees its job as making people fit the system will not be capable of doing the work outlined in this book. This general orientation of the service

should include an expressed commitment to providing support for people who behave in socially unacceptable ways.

EVIDENCE OF COMPETENCE

- These ideas should be present in the service's documentation about its overall purpose.
- When you ask staff about the main philosophy of the service, you should hear these ideas.
- When you ask about successes the service has had and some of the things that have been hard, you should hear the same ideas with a clear indication of standing by people and working through their crises and difficulties.

(2) A track record in working with significant behaviours

The service should see itself as having some kind of commitment to people whose behaviour gives rise to concern.

EVIDENCE OF COMPETENCE

- When you ask for specific examples about the behavioural work of the service, these should be readily forthcoming.
- There should be evidence of people using the service whose behaviour had/has been of concern for some long time (that is, the service will stand by people over time).

(3) Knowledge about autism (or a commitment to learn)

The service should be up to date in understanding the nature of autism and the practical implications of current understandings. There should be regular staff training, specialized consultancy input or involvement with an autism-specific accreditation scheme. If not already in place, there should be concrete plans to provide such inputs.

EVIDENCE OF COMPETENCE

- Any staff member that you ask will be able to explain autism and how it affects the way the person is supported.

- ○ The training record will indicate all staff accessing autism-specific training.
- ○ There will be evident certain key practices which are detailed below – good organization, good structure and visual back up for all communications geared to conveying information to the users of the service.

(4) Generally well organized

The service will be clear about what it is doing and why it is doing it and convey a sense of purpose. There will be an active atmosphere but not one marked by rushing and apparent chaos. It will be reliable in delivering what it offers.

EVIDENCE OF COMPETENCE

- ○ Any staff member that you ask will be able to explain clearly what he or she will be doing that week.
- ○ There will be available timetables and plans that tally with what you see going on.
- ○ When there is a changeover in activity you will observe this being given time, with care taken to inform and prepare people for the change.

(5) A high level of structure

As well as being well organized, planned and relevant activities will fill the vast majority of the time. The range of activities is perhaps less critical than the fact that there is always the option to engage in something and there are not long periods when people are left to their own devices. There will also be clear rules about what is and is not acceptable behaviour.

EVIDENCE OF COMPETENCE

- ○ The activities that you see any individual involved in will be personally relevant to that individual.

- It will be clear on observation that most of the people that you see are engaged in a relevant activity for most of the time. You will not observe people spending a lot of time 'waiting' or just sitting around.
- Rules for behaviour will be posted or you will hear verbal reference to such rules whenever limits are set upon a behaviour.

(6) Use of visual supports for informative communication

The service will understand that using a range of visual back ups will increase the access of people to necessary information.

EVIDENCE OF COMPETENCE

- You will observe all information giving to service users being backed up with some kind of visual support. You will see and hear reference to schedules or timetables when activities change.
- Explanations of where someone is going or what they are going to do will include reference to pictures, symbols or the written word.
- Social rules will be publicly posted in pictures and words or carried on cue cards by individuals.
- Start and end point of tasks will be marked in a visual way (start and finish boxes, tasks in worksheet format, egg timers or drawn clock faces to indicate duration and/or transitions).
- Staff and service users will carry visual communication supports (wallets and cue cards, pictures on key rings or ring binders, writing pads/palmtops and pens).

(7) Oriented to quality of life not just behaviour

The service, if a school/college, will have a broad and balanced curriculum which covers the same areas as the curriculum followed by other children in the society. In the case of an adult service, the focus will be upon supporting people into the kind of life that will work best for them.

EVIDENCE OF COMPETENCE

- The written plans for individuals will cover a range of areas, not just behaviours, those areas reflecting the general curriculum or a person-centred plan which has looked at the whole person and identified the key elements in a positive, individualized lifestyle.

- When you observe the service in action you will see people pursuing well-planned activities (see above) which have clear personal meaning or for which a clear rationale can be provided.

- You will not see people sitting around doing nothing.

(8) A coherent approach to working positively to reduce behaviours causing justifiable concern

As well as a general commitment to people whose behaviour causes concern the service will have clear procedures for assessing behaviour, identifying relevant interventions, implementing the interventions and monitoring progress. Staff will seem to know what they are doing.

EVIDENCE OF COMPETENCE

- The service will have a specific policy that provides an overview of its approach to problematic behaviours. This policy will include the value base, the principles guiding practice, the operational procedures for planning, implementing and monitoring interventions, examples of acceptable and unacceptable interventions and what to do in case of complaint.

- You will be able to see a range of assessment formats that the service uses, examples of written intervention plans and the graphs that are used to monitor progress.

- There will be a staff training policy that outlines the training the service offers its staff and a training log that indicates how many staff have been through the training relevant to the behavioural work of the service. When you ask staff about the programmes and guidelines that they are following for an individual they will, at the very least, be able to explain what these are – even better, they will be able to explain why and how they have been chosen.

(9) A coherent, well-thought-out approach to managing dangerous incidents

The service will acknowledge that sometimes dangerous incidents occur and will have a professional and respectful approach to these occurrences.

EVIDENCE OF COMPETENCE

- The service will have a specific policy that provides an overview of its approach to 'crisis management' (it may be part of an overall behaviour policy or a separate policy). This will cover its value base, the principles guiding its practice including clear reference to prevention, diffusion and redirection, the operational procedures for planning, implementing and monitoring strategies, examples of acceptable and unacceptable practice and what to do in case of complaint.

- You will be able to see a risk assessment format and written individual procedures that include how to avoid, defuse or redirect incidents as well as what to do when a dangerous behaviour actually occurs.

- In the staff training policy there will be reference to the training that the service offers its staff in this area and the training log will indicate that all except the most recently recruited staff have been through this training.

- If you are present when an incident occurs you will observe it being managed without signs of panic and with no shouting other than that required to draw the attention of others to danger and to summon needed help.

(10) A collaborative rather than an authoritarian style

The service will live the ethic of respect, involvement and team work at every level.

EVIDENCE OF COMPETENCE

- The documented operational procedures will indicate how those using the service, their family and friends and the staff working with the people most of the time are involved in the decision making.

- When you ask any service user, who is able to give you an answer that you will understand, the reason why particular programmes and guidelines are being followed it will be explained in ways that indicate involvement in the process rather than 'I was told to'.

- When you observe the service in action you will see staff interacting with the people that they are supporting for a considerable proportion of the time.

- Social interaction between staff and those using the service will be as much about general social engagement as about giving instructions and setting limits.

(11) Low staff turnover

Staff turnover should be less than 50 per cent in a year. Whilst this is an arbitrary figure it is there as a reminder that the patient, respectful and sometimes fraught work that is at the heart of this book is simply not possible in a service that cannot retain its staff.

Concluding remarks

Any system needs to be monitored and reviewed regularly. This is particularly true when considering long-term support, sometimes in the face of very difficult circumstances, where consistency and continuity are vital to efficacy. We have highlighted some of the key areas of service functioning that support the likelihood of good quality behavioural work. It is a start but there will be other criteria that need to be added. We have been careful not to mention resources, particularly staffing levels. This is not because we think it unimportant but because we think it more important to clarify what needs to be done rather than start from the idea that there is some ideal staffing ratio. What can be stated unequivocally is that any way of providing for people whose behaviour causes serious concern will require substantial resources, resources that include high staffing levels. What can be stated with equal certainty is that it costs no more to provide a service well than it costs to provide it badly. What can be stated with even more certainty is that people with autism are not the only ones whose behaviour may cause concern. The behaviour of carers, educators, supporters, managers, planners and policy makers needs as much attention as does the behaviour of the person with autism who is identified as 'behaviourally challenging'.

Autism – Supporters' Help to Explore the Difficulties

This is a problem-solving job aide not a developed assessment. It is meant to show the major impacts of what we mean by autism for an individual. It is to help refine what is meant by the diagnosis, inform better our understanding of behavioural issues and contribute to the setting of priorities in support for the individual.

Go through each section and circle the rating that you think best applies to the person that you know. Transfer the individual ratings to the summary profile chart at the end.

A. Difficulties in understanding

Social Information

Includes difficulties in understanding the meaning of other people's facial expressions, difficulties in giving information (too much or too little), difficulties in adjusting behaviour that the person knows causes distress to others, not initiating with others to tell them (by gesture, word, sign, picture) what your wants/needs are.

5. A VERY SIGNIFICANT IMPACT ON EVERYDAY LIFE

Seems to lack all understanding of other people; does not register how they are; does not seem to realize that other people can be helpful; seems lost in own world and to take no account of others, may perhaps just treat them as like other physical objects in the world.

4. A SIGNIFICANT IMPACT ON EVERYDAY LIFE

Does initiate to other people about wants/needs at least some of the time but will often initiate in a clumsy, odd or aggressive way; does not really understand distress in others and may seem to deliberately do things that cause distress.

3. AN IMPACT ON EVERYDAY LIFE

Has many good ways of interacting with others but still makes mistakes that upset others or cause them to reject the individual.

2. A SMALL IMPACT ON EVERYDAY LIFE

1. NO IMPACT AT ALL ON EVERYDAY LIFE / NOT AN ISSUE FOR THIS PERSON

Understanding language

Includes near complete inability to get information from the speech of others, significant hearing losses, ability to get information from the speech of others but only at a slow rate so that the individual is easily overwhelmed by speech, a good ability to understand but always at a literal and concrete level.

5. A VERY SIGNIFICANT IMPACT ON EVERYDAY LIFE

Is almost completely unable to get any meaning from the speech of others. At best may follow everyday instructions given in context.

4. A SIGNIFICANT IMPACT ON EVERYDAY LIFE

Can follow everyday instructions and may be able to understand rather more but takes a lot of time to process verbal information and gets overwhelmed/upset by too much speech so that in practice only a very limited amount of information is taken in.

3. AN IMPACT ON EVERYDAY LIFE

Has generally good understanding of familiar information but does take time to process so that care is needed to present information in manageable chunks. Still needs to experience situations in order to learn about them – cannot really prepare for things by 'having them explained'.

2. A SMALL IMPACT ON EVERYDAY LIFE

1. NO IMPACT AT ALL ON EVERYDAY LIFE / NOT AN ISSUE FOR THIS PERSON

Understanding time lapse/event sequences

Involves difficulties in really understanding when important events will happen so that can only be given information just before an event happens, constant worrying about when he is to do certain things or when certain people will be around (a lot of when questions), generally good understanding of what is said but great difficulty when given a sequence of things to do (tends to mix up the order).

5. A VERY SIGNIFICANT IMPACT ON EVERYDAY LIFE

Great care has to be taken in preparing for upcoming events and this is an important day-to-day issue (not just about occasional events). The worrying about 'when' is constant. Information about event sequences can only be given over very short time frames (for example, what will happen in the next hour rather than what we are doing today or this week).

4. A SIGNIFICANT IMPACT ON EVERYDAY LIFE

Care does have to be taken in preparing for events but this is mainly around occasional, out of the ordinary events. There is worrying about 'when' every day but it is not intense and hard to distract from. Can understand event sequences for no more than one day at a time.

3. AN IMPACT ON EVERYDAY LIFE

Can be prepared for events at least a day in advance but no more. There is some worrying about 'when' but it is not every day. Although generally well able to understand things, does get into difficulty when it is important to remember the sequence of what is said.

2. A SMALL IMPACT ON EVERYDAY LIFE

1. NO IMPACT AT ALL ON EVERYDAY LIFE / NOT AN ISSUE FOR THIS PERSON

B. Difficulties in self expression

Self-awareness – understanding personal feelings/wants/needs

Seems to get upset and know that something needs doing but does not seem to know what it is (for example, may lead you around, getting more and more upset but not seem to know what it is she wants). Has general difficulty in reporting on feelings – will respond to questions about how she is feeling with answers that seem out of line with what you can observe the person to be experiencing (for example, will say she is happy, although as far as you can see she seems very upset in some way). Can report on feelings but often unable/makes errors in judging what has caused those feelings. Can show unusual responses to pain – definitely feels pain but will sometimes have things happen that are clearly painful but seem to have no impact.

5. A VERY SIGNIFICANT IMPACT ON EVERYDAY LIFE

On most days gets in distress but without seeming to know why. Has a history of serious medical problems which she has not reported although in general is well able to report on pain and discomfort and the reasons for it.

4. A SIGNIFICANT IMPACT ON EVERYDAY LIFE

Sometimes gets in distress without seeming to know why but at other times can identify the reasons. Can report on emotional feelings but cannot identify what has caused those feelings and cannot explain why she did what she did if she acted out those feelings.

3. AN IMPACT ON EVERYDAY LIFE

Is good at identifying general wants and needs and can sometimes identify what has caused emotional feelings such as happiness, anger or sadness. Not good at understanding the links between emotional feelings and own behaviour – does not give plausible explanations when asked why certain behaviours occurred.

2. A SMALL IMPACT ON EVERYDAY LIFE

1. NO IMPACT AT ALL ON EVERYDAY LIFE / NOT AN ISSUE FOR THIS PERSON

Awareness of need to communicate

Is aware of own wants and needs and will work hard to sort them out but does not communicate with others to get them involved in the process – will always try to work it out on his own. Also included here difficulties in using communication for any other purpose than to satisfy immediate wants and needs – thus although he communicates about wants and needs, does not communicate in terms of sharing information and general conversation.

5. A VERY SIGNIFICANT IMPACT ON EVERYDAY LIFE

Never initiates any form of communication with others.

4. A SIGNIFICANT IMPACT ON EVERYDAY LIFE

Will sometimes initiate communication about some immediate wants/needs but not very often and would always prefer to sort things out for himself.

3. AN IMPACT ON EVERYDAY LIFE

Will generally communicate if wants something and cannot get it for himself but never initiates communication for any other purpose.

2. A SMALL IMPACT ON EVERYDAY LIFE

1. NO IMPACT AT ALL ON EVERYDAY LIFE / NOT AN ISSUE FOR THIS PERSON

Difficulties with the means of communicating

This extends from the complete absence of any kind of recognizable communication skill, to having limited means of symbolic expression (words, signs, icons, pictures), to having good symbolic skills but sometimes difficulty in finding the right word/symbol.

5. A VERY SIGNIFICANT IMPACT ON EVERYDAY LIFE

Has no means of communicating with others in ways that they are likely to understand. At best those who know the person well understand the meanings of certain sounds, looks, movements but a newcomer would not be able to read these meanings.

4. A SIGNIFICANT IMPACT ON EVERYDAY LIFE

Has some basic gestures such as leading others to things. May be able to point or uses a small number of meaningful words, signs, icons, pictures but can only communicate about a very few things and cannot put together sequences of symbols.

3. AN IMPACT ON EVERYDAY LIFE

Has a range of symbols that she can use and this is generally adequate for communicating about everyday wants and needs. May be able to put together sequences of symbols but it is mainly about immediate concerns. We would count in here people who are sometimes able to communicate in complex ways but often run into word-finding difficulty so that in practice their communication breaks down often.

2. A SMALL IMPACT ON EVERYDAY LIFE

1. NO IMPACT AT ALL ON EVERYDAY LIFE / NOT AN ISSUE FOR THIS PERSON

C. Problems in thinking

Problem-solving

Included here are difficulties in imaginative activities, problems in coping with unstructured times, problems in dealing with unfamiliar situations that arise and difficulties in making choices.

5. A VERY SIGNIFICANT IMPACT ON EVERYDAY LIFE

Has no imaginative play and does not access symbolic media such as books and videos. Cannot cope at all with unstructured times and must have activities organized and directions provided at all times. Cannot cope at all with unfamiliar situations and cannot cope with being offered choices.

4. A SIGNIFICANT IMPACT ON EVERYDAY LIFE

Does access some symbolic media. Can find ways of filling unstructured times but not for very long and not all the time. Can sometimes find ways of solving problems (for example, finding where a drink is) but not always. Can cope with some choices but only if presented in a two choice format with both items visible.

3. AN IMPACT ON EVERYDAY LIFE

Can organize own time but for no more than an hour or two (could not organize to fill a weekend). Will sort out everyday problems in familiar environments but could not be relied on to always do this. Can cope with choices between three and four items but cannot deal with open-ended choices ('what do you want?').

2. A SMALL IMPACT ON EVERYDAY LIFE

1. NO IMPACT AT ALL ON EVERYDAY LIFE / NOT AN ISSUE FOR THIS PERSON

Tightly focused attention

Included here is the exclusive focus on a single topic/activity to the exclusion of all else, or at the other extreme the complete inability to handle a lot of stimulation present simultaneously – it is part of the same problem of being able to process several items of information in a prioritized fashion.

5. A VERY SIGNIFICANT IMPACT ON EVERYDAY LIFE

All transitions (stopping one thing, starting another) are difficult. It is very hard to distract from any topic or activity on to which attention has been locked. In many ordinary situations the individual gets overwhelmed by the amount of stimulation.

4. A SIGNIFICANT IMPACT ON EVERYDAY LIFE

Transitions can be made but they always require careful management. Likewise it is possible to distract but time and care are always needed. Copes with most everyday situations but easily overwhelmed in new situations.

3. AN IMPACT ON EVERYDAY LIFE

Transitions and distractions generally managed well but still depends on a TEACCH type system for this. Will sometimes get very stuck and find it hard to move on and is sometimes overwhelmed by stimulation.

2. A SMALL IMPACT ON EVERYDAY LIFE

1. NO IMPACT AT ALL ON EVERYDAY LIFE/ NOT AN ISSUE FOR THIS PERSON

Binary thinking

Judges situations in very categorical ways with no gradations ('grayscale'). Cannot tolerate making mistakes, things not being just as he wants them, being corrected, losing at games.

5. A VERY SIGNIFICANT IMPACT ON EVERYDAY LIFE

On most days there are confrontation about things not being just as they are wanted, people not doing exactly what they are supposed to do, making mistakes, losing. In general those around the person feel that they are walking on eggs.

4. A SIGNIFICANT IMPACT ON EVERYDAY LIFE

There are regular difficulties around these issues, perhaps not every day but certainly every week.

3. AN IMPACT ON ESVERYDAY LIFE

The individual is beginning to learn to tolerate making mistakes and being corrected but care is still needed about this. Likewise can sometimes cope with losing and things/people not being exactly as they should be.

2. A SMALL IMPACT ON EVERYDAY LIFE

I. NO IMPACT AT ALL ON EVERYDAY LIFE/ NOT AN ISSUE FOR THIS PERSON

Perseveration

The difficulty is getting stuck repeating a behaviour of some kind and getting more distressed as the repetition goes on. The person may show signs of trying to stop the behaviour themselves (for example, banging their head to make thoughts go away, self-restraining their hands) and the person will usually be relieved if they are forcefully stopped and moved on.

5. A VERY SIGNIFICANT IMPACT ON EVERYDAY LIFE

On most days this issue arises — there is distress and intrusive interventions used to move the person on.

4. A SIGNIFICANT IMPACT ON EVERYDAY LIFE

There are regular difficulties around these issues, perhaps not every day but certainly every week.

3. AN IMPACT ON EVERYDAY LIFE

This does occur and needs to be considered in the support plans for the individual but it is not a major area of concern.

2. A SMALL IMPACT ON EVERYDAY LIFE

I. NO IMPACT AT ALL ON EVERYDAY LIFE / NOT AN ISSUE FOR THIS PERSON

D. Personal sensations – sensory, physical and emotional difficulties

Sensory modulation and phobias

This covers the distress caused by specific sensory experiences and specific feared objects (phobias).

5. A VERY SIGNIFICANT IMPACT ON EVERYDAY LIFE

On most days there is distress around these issues. The person has or is thought to have multiple sensory stressors and in different domains (sound, touch, taste, sight, smell).

4. A SIGNIFICANT IMPACT ON EVERYDAY LIFE

There are a small number of sensory stressors but these do occur regularly and always have to be thought of in planning things for the person. The person may have a specific phobia (for example, dogs, wind) and these require accommodation when making plans.

3. AN IMPACT ON EVERYDAY LIFE

There are known stressors and/or phobias but the individual generally copes well but it still means that certain ordinary situations are avoided if possible.

2. A SMALL IMPACT ON EVERYDAY LIFE

1. NO IMPACT AT ALL ON EVERYDAY LIFE / NOT AN ISSUE FOR THIS PERSON

Physical well being

This covers both general health (resistance to infection) and recurring specific health problems such as ear infections, dental problems, sinus problems, bowel problems.

5. A VERY SIGNIFICANT IMPACT ON EVERYDAY LIFE

There are always concerns about the person's health and frequent medical consultations. The person is under constant or frequent treatment (for example, antibiotics, laxatives, allergy meds).

4. A SIGNIFICANT IMPACT ON EVERYDAY LIFE

There are recurring phases of ill health but clear phases of positive, good health can be identified in between. Repeated treatment is needed but, again, there are treatment free periods.

3. AN IMPACT ON EVERYDAY LIFE

The individual is known over time to have a vulnerability to particular health problems (for example, ear infections, bowel problems). All those supporting the person need to know about this issue. These problems may arise three to six times a year. However most of the time the person sustains good health.

2. A SMALL IMPACT ON EVERYDAY LIFE

1. NO IMPACT AT ALL ON EVERYDAY LIFE/ NOT AN ISSUE FOR THIS PERSON

Emotional well being

This covers the tendency always to process negative information/experiences but ignore positives; intense bursts of negative emotionality; general tendencies to get over-aroused and out of control; extended phases of low mood, lack of tolerance, irritability, withdrawal sometimes recurring ('cyclical') sometimes as part of a 'one off' breakdown.

5. A VERY SIGNIFICANT IMPACT ON EVERYDAY LIFE

On a daily basis the individual dwells on negative things and becomes intensely distressed. There are daily occurrences of intense emotional outbursts. The person is recognized as being in a phase of loss of well being and medication is being used/considered to address this. Any or all of these are leading to the individual's life being much more restricted than it otherwise would be and support plans focus heavily on this area.

4. A SIGNIFICANT IMPACT ON EVERYDAY LIFE

The person is clearly not enjoying life as much as they normally do. Negative processing biases are evident on a daily basis, moods are often negative and intense and there are three to four major outbursts a week. There may be signs of an extended down phase and there are some restrictions on the person's life. Support plans focus on this area and medication is being considered but not yet used.

3. AN IMPACT ON EVERYDAY LIFE

The above problems are clearly a cause for concern and a focus for support plans. Whilst the individual is not enjoying life as much as she might, the difficulties are not leading to actual restrictions in her life.

2. A SMALL IMPACT ON EVERYDAY LIFE

1. NO IMPACT ON EVERYDAY LIFE / NOT AN ISSUE FOR THIS PERSON

E. Control of physical movements

This covers general clumsiness, the tendency to make eye-catching body movements (aka 'stereotypies'), the adoption of fixed, frozen postures and apparent movements that occur outside the person's control and that they make obvious efforts to inhibit (for example, self-restraining).

5. A VERY SIGNIFICANT IMPACT ON EVERYDAY LIFE

Movement problems are evident every day, definitely interfere with the person's life and are the focus of specific support plans. This will usually be because the person is spending a lot of time on 'stereotypies', is often getting stuck and needing help to move on or is having frequent movements that appear out of control and have a major impact (for example, leading to injury of the self and others).

4. A SIGNIFICANT IMPACT ON EVERYDAY LIFE

Movement issues are a source of concern and a focus of support plans. They arise several times a week but there can be days where these issues do not arise.

3. AN IMPACT ON EVERYDAY LIFE

This is a known area of need and everyone who supports the person has to be aware of the issues. There is some impact on the person's quality of life but this is limited provided that support plans for these issues are followed.

2. A SMALL IMPACT ON EVERYDAY LIFE

1. NO IMPACT ON EVERYDAY LIFE / NOT AN ISSUE FOR THIS PERSON

A – SHED SUMMARY PROFILE	
AREA	**RATING**
DIFFICULTIES IN UNDERSTANDING – Social information	
DIFFICULTIES IN UNDERSTANDING – Language	
DIFFICULTIES IN UNDERSTANDING – Time lapse/event sequences	
DIFFICULTIES IN SELF EXPRESSION – Personal feelings/wants/needs	
DIFFICULTIES IN SELF EXPRESSION – Need to communicate	
DIFFICULTIES IN SELF EXPRESSION – Means of communicating	
PROBLEMS IN THINKING – Problem-solving	
PROBLEMS IN THINKING – Tightly focused attention	
PROBLEMS IN THINKING – Binary thinking	
PROBLEMS IN THINKING – Perseveration	
PERSONAL SENSATIONS – SENSORY, PHYSICAL, EMOTIONAL DIFFICULTIES – Sensory modulation and phobias	
Physical well being	
Emotional well being	
CONTROL OF PHYSICAL MOVEMENTS	

Appendix II
Identifying Factors Involved in a Behaviour which Gives Cause for Concern

This checklist is intended to be a simple aide to help build a story around a person's behaviour. It is not a formal assessment tool but a way of helping you to organize the information you already hold about the person and their behaviour. It may also help you to identify gaps in your knowledge which might need further exploration. Answer each section as comprehensively as you can. Ask other people who know the person well. This should help you identify the various areas in which the person may need to be supported around their behaviour, including steps which can be taken to avoid or reduce the behaviour in the immediate and long term. Use the information gathered here to help you draw up your behaviour support plan.

Name of the person   **Date the information was gathered**

1. Define clearly the behaviour of concern (state what exactly the person does, what precise form the behaviour takes).

2. State why the behaviour has been identified as problematic (what costs are involved and to whom).

3. Identify the function(s) of the behaviour (there may be more than one). Does the behaviour appear to achieve something for the person, on at least some occasions?

Possible functions are

i. Access to something important (for example, some form of social attention; a particularly activity; stimulation; sensory enjoyment; food or drink; satisfaction).

ii. Avoidance or termination of something unwanted (for example, social attention; a particular activity; specific or general demands or requests; unpleasant sensory input; pain or discomfort).

iii. Relief of high levels of emotion/arousal (NB. sometimes the behaviour occurs when there is high emotion or arousal but the person does not seem to relieved by this).

4. Specify what you would like the person to be doing instead of the behaviour of concern.

Constructive alternatives might be

i. Another way of achieving the needs and wants identified above (access, escape/termination, relief).

ii. The use of a self-control skill.

○ Does the person already have the alternative skill(s) you have identified? YES / NO

○ If yes, are these alternative skills consistently reinforced – are they always successful in achieving their desired outcome? YES / NO

○ If the person does not have the alternative skills, would it be reasonable to try to teach this skill to the person? YES / NO

5. List out the things which seem directly to trigger the behaviour. These may be

    i. External events – (for example, sensory stimuli such as noise, sights, smells, texture, touch, heat; specific people; specific request or demands; denials or prohibitions; specific events occurring).

    ii. Internal events – (for example, a pain, a memory, an interpretation).

    iii. Unknown events.

6. Are there circumstances when the behaviour is more likely to occur or when the person is more likely to react adversely to the triggers identified above?

    i. When certain internal factors operate (for example, when the person is tired, unwell, unhappy, anxious, depressed).

    ii. When particular external factors operate (for example, is the behaviour more likely in particular places, at particular times, in the presence of particular people, during particular activities).

7.   Are there any recent or ongoing life events (for example, losses, changes, accidents, illnesses) which may be affecting the person's well being and reducing their ability to cope with day-to-day pressures? List these out & state how they might be affecting well being.

8.   What are the person's likes? Are these likes available to the person on a regular basis? If the answer is 'no' how might this be related to the person's current behaviour.

9.   What is the person's preferred lifestyle (for example, busy, structured, relaxed, stimulating, noisy, active)? Is the current lifestyle compatible with the person's preferred lifestyle? If the answer is 'no' how might this be related to the person's current behaviour.

10. Does the person have specific difficulties in processing information which may increase their vulnerability to use the behaviour of concern (see Appendix 1)? What are these difficulties?

Constructive Behavioural Support –
Service Evaluation Guide

This guide is based upon the text of Chapter 14 and should be used in conjunction with that chapter. It is a way of looking at the strengths and needs of a service in terms of doing the kind of work outlined in this book. It is not a comprehensive guide to service evaluation!!

Key areas of service functioning are rated using a scale with a 5 point range – this is just to make it easier to 'see at a glance' where the strengths and needs lie. No detailed interpretation can be made of exact scores. Nor is it necessary to decide on an exact score – if you want to rate between the numerical anchor points, feel free!

For the first 10 rating areas the anchor points are defined as follows

  1   No evidence of this

  2   Some, but not much, evidence of this

  3   Some evidence of this

  4   Clear evidence of this

  5   Very clear evidence of this

For the 11th rating area (staff turnover) the points are defined on the scale itself.

Rating Areas

A general philosophy that is respectful and inclusive

1	2	3	4	5

A track record of working with significant behaviours

1	2	3	4	5

Knowledge about autism or a commitment to learn

1	2	3	4	5

Generally well organized

1	2	3	4	5

A high level of structure

1	2	3	4	5

Use of visual supports for informative communication

1	2	3	4	5

The service is oriented to quality of life, not just behaviour

1	2	3	4	5

There is a coherent approach to working positively to reduce behaviours causing justifiable concern

1	2	3	4	5

There is a coherent, well-thought-out approach to managing dangerous incidents

1	2	3	4	5

The style is collaborative rather than authoritarian

1	2	3	4	5

Staff turnover is

1	2	3	4	5
>65%pa	50–65%pa	35–50%pa	20–35%pa	<20%pa

Bibliography

Print references relevant to autism

Adams, J.I. (1997) *Autism – P.D.D. More Creative Ideas (from age eight to early adulthood)*. Arlington, TX: Future Horizons.

Attwood, T. (1997) *Asperger's Syndrome: A Guide for Parents and Professionals*. London: Jessica Kingsley.

Ayres, J.A. (1979) *Sensory Integration and the Child*. Los Angeles, CA: Western Psychology Services.

Bailey, A., Phillips, W. and Rutter, M. (1996) Autism: Towards an integration of clinical, genetic, neuropsychological, and neurobiological perspectives. *Journal of Child Psychology and Psychiatry, 37*, 1, 89–126.

Baron-Cohen, S. (1995) *Mindblindness: An essay on autism and theory of mind*. Cambridge, MA: MIT Press/Bradford Books

Bondy, A. and Frost, L. (1994) The picture exchange communication system. *Focus on Autistic Behavior, 9*, 1–19.

Carr, E.G., Horner, R.H., Turnbull, A.P and Colleagues (1999) *Positive Behaviour Support for People with Developmental Disabilities. A Research Synthesis*. Washington: AAMR.

Carr, E.G., Levin, L., McConnachie, G., Carlson, J.I., Kemp, D.C., Smith, C.E. (1994) *Communication-Based Intervention for Problem Behavior*. Baltimore: Paul H. Brookes.

Clements, J. (1997) 'Challenging needs and problematic behavior.' In J. O'Hara and A. Sperlinger (eds) *Adults with Learning Disabilities. A Practical Approach for Health Professionals*. Chichester: John Wiley and Sons

Clements, J. (1997) 'Sustaining a cognitive psychology for people with learning disabilities'. In B. Stenfert Kroese, D. Dagnan and K. Loumidis (eds) *Cognitive Behaviour Therapy for People with Learning Disabilities*. London: Routledge.

Cumine, V., Leach, J. And Stevenson, G. (1998) *Asperger Syndrome. A practical guide for teachers*. London: David Fulton.

Emerson, E. (1995) *Challenging behaviour: Analysis and intervention in people with Learning Disabilities*. Cambridge: Cambridge University Press.

Fouse, B. and Wheeler, M. (1997) *A Treasure Chest of Behavioral Strategies for Individuals with Autism*. Arlington,TX: Future Horizons.

Frith, U. (1989) *Autism: Explaining the Enigma*. Oxford: Blackwell.

Frith, U. (ed.) (1991*) Autism and Asperger Syndrome*. Cambridge: Cambridge University Press.

Gazzaniga, M.S. (1998) *The Mind's Past.* Berkeley and Los Angeles: University of California Press.

Grandin, T. (1996) *Thinking in Pictures.* New York: Vintage Books.

Gray, C. (1994a) *Comic Strip Conversations.* Jenison Public Schools, Jenison, Michigan.

Gray, C. (1994b) *The New Social Story Book.* Arlington, TX: Future Horizons.

Hamilton-Ely, S.P. (1990) The Options Method. *Communication, 24,* 6–7.

Happe, F. (1994) *Autism. An Introduction to Psychological Theory.* London: UCL Press.

Harris, J., Allen, D., Cornick, M., Jefferson, A., Mills, R. (1996) *Physical Interventions. A Policy Framework.* Plymouth: Bild publications.

Harris, P.L. (1994) The child's understanding of emotion: Developmental change and the family environment. *Journal of Child Psychology and Psychiatry, 35,* 1, 3–28.

Hay, D.F. (1994) Prosocial development. *Journal of Child Psychology and Psychiatry, 35,* 1, 29–72.

Hodgson, L.A. (1998*) Visual Strategies for Improving Communication. Volume 1: Practical Supports for School and Home.* Michigan: Quirk Roberts.

Howlin, P. (1997) *Autism: Preparing for Adulthood.* London: Routledge.

Howlin, P. (1997) Prognosis in autism: Do specialist treatments affect long-term outcome? *European Child and Adolescent Psychiatry, 6,* 55–72.

Howlin, P. (1998) Psychological and educational treatments for autism. *Journal of Child Psychology and Psychiatry, 39,* 3, 307–322.

Howlin, P. and Yates, P. (1999) The potential effectiveness of social skills groups for adults with autism. *Autism, 3,* 3, 299–307.

Howlin, P., Baron-Cohen, S. and Hadwin, J. (1999) *Teaching Children with Autism to Mind Read.* Chichester: Wiley.

Jordan, R. and Powell, S. (1995*) Understanding and Teaching Children with Autism.* Chichester: Wiley.

King, L. (1991) Sensory integration: An effective approach to therapy and education. *Autism Research Review International, 5* (2).

Lanconi, G.E. and O'Reilly, M.F. (1998) A review of research on physical exercise with people with severe and profound developmental disabilities. *Research in Developmental Disabilities 19,* 1, 477–492.

Lee, A. and Hobson, R.P. (1998) On developing self concepts: A controlled study of children and adolescents with autism. *Journal of Child Psychology and Psychiatry, 39,* 8, 1131–1144.

Mesibov, G.B. (1997) Formal and informal measures on the effectiveness of the TEACCH program. *Autism, 1,* 1, 25–35.

Nind, M. and Hewett, D. (1988) Interaction as curriculum. *British Journal of Special Education, 15,* 2, 55–57.

O'Neill, R.E. Horner, R.H., Albin, R.W., Sprague, J.R., Storey, K. and Newton, J.S. (1997) *Functional Assessment and Program Development for Problem Behavior. A Practical Handbook.* Brooks/Cole: Pacific Grove

Parsons, S. and Mitchell, P. (1999) What children with autism understand about thoughts and thought bubbles. *Autism, 39,* 1, 17–38.

Pennington, B. and Ozonoff, S. (1996) Executive functions and developmental psychopathology. *Journal of Child Psychology and Psychiatry, 37,* 1, 51–88.

Quill, K.A. (1997) Instructional considerations for young children with autism: The rationale for visually cued instruction. *Journal of Autism and Developmental Disorders, 27,* 6, 697–714.

Rimland, B. (1988) Physical exercise and autism. *Autism Research Review International, 23.*

Rimland, B. and Edelson, S.M. (1995) Brief report: A pilot study of auditory integration training in autism. *Journal of Autism and Developmental Disorders, 25,* 61–70.

Schopler, E. (1995) (ed) *Parent Survival Manual.* New York/ London: Plenum.

Schopler, E., Mesibov, G.B. and Hearsey, K. (1995) Structured teaching in the TEACCH system. In E. Schopler and G. Mesibov (eds) *Learning and Cognition in Autism.* New York: Plenum Press.

Schopler, E., Mesibov, G.B. and Kunce, L.J. (1998) *Asperger Syndrome or High Functioning Autism.* New York: Plenum Press.

Singh, N. (1997) *Prevention and Treatment of Severe Behavior Problems: Models and Methods in Developmental Disabilities.* Pacific Grove: Brooks/Cole

Thayer, R.E. (1996) *The Origin of Everyday Moods.* Oxford: Oxford University Press

Williams, D. (1992) *Nobody Nowhere.* London: Jessica Kingsley.

Zarkowska, E. and Clements, J. (1994) *Problem Behaviour and People with Severe Learning Disabilities.* London: Chapman and Hall.

Web references relevant to autism

There is a huge amount of material about autism on the world wide web…and it changes all the time. So it is worth searching. Here are some useful starting points

http://www.autism-society.org

(web site of the Autism Society of America)

http://www.oneworld.org/autismuk/index.html

(web site of England's National Autistic Society)

http://members.tripod.com/~transmil/alp.htm

(a site providing links to many other autism sites)

http://www.udel.edu/bkirby/asperger

(lots of useful stuff about Asperger's Syndrome/high functioning autism)

http://www.feat.org/featnews

(a daily newsletter compiling autism relevant scientific, political and human interest items)

Person centred planning – a very useful web site

www.allenshea.com

Index